King Driftwood

ROBERT MINHINNICK was born in 1952 and lives in south Wales. He has been the winner of a Society of Authors Eric Gregory Award and a Cholmondeley Award, and has twice won the Forward Prize for best individual poem, while his books of essays have twice won the Wales Book of the Year Prize. Robert Minhinnick edited *Poetry Wales* magazine from 1997 to 2008. His first novel, *Sea Holly* (Seren) was shortlisted for the 2008 Royal Society of Literature's Ondaatje Prize. He is an advisor to the environmental charity Sustainable Wales.

T0164454

Also by Robert Minhinnick from Carcanet Press

Selected Poems
After the Hurricane: New Poems

As editor and translator
The Adulterer's Tongue: Six Welsh Poets

ROBERT MINHINNICK

King Driftwood

CARCANET

First published in Great Britain in 2008 by
Carcanet Press Limited
Alliance House
Cross Street
Manchester M2 7AQ

A CIP catalogue record for this book is available from the British Library
ISBN 978 1 85754 965 2

The publisher acknowledges financial assistance from Arts Council England

Typeset by XL Publishing Services, Tiverton
Printed and bound in England by SRP Ltd, Exeter

Contents

Acknowledgements

Some of these poems have appeared in the following magazines and anthologies:

The Manhattan Review; *New Welsh Review*; *PN Review*; *Planet*; *Poetry London*; *Poetry Review*; *Poetry Wales*; *Pratik* (Nepal), *The Wolf.*

After the First Death: Wales and War in the Twentieth Century (Seren, ed. Tony Curtis); Alhambra Poetry Calendar, 2007, 2008; *Answering Back* (Picador, ed. Carol Ann Duffy); *The Forward Book of Poetry* 2004, 2005; *Light Unlocked: Christmas Card Poems* (Enitharmon, eds. Kevin Crossley-Holland and Lawrence Sail); *The Ropes: Poems to Hold On To* (Diamond Twig); *100 Poets Against the War* (Salt, ed. Todd Swift); *180 More Extraordinary Poems for Every Day* (Random House, ed. Billy Collins).

'The Fox in the National Museum of Wales' won the Forward Prize for best individual poem in 2003. 'The Castaway' was shortlisted for this award in 2004.

Thanks go to Volcano Theatre Company for commissioning the play *A Few Little Drops* (2007) from which various writings are published here.

A small selection of these poems, in English and Italian, translated by Andrea Bianchi and Silvana Siviero, appears in *La Rossa Amica* (Mobydick) 2007.

Recordings of several of these poems are available via Poetry Archive – www.poetryarchive.org

The Fox in the National Museum of Wales

He scans the frames but doesn't stop,
the fox who has come to the museum today,
his eye in the Renaissance
and his brush in the Baroque.

Between dynasties his footprints
have still to fade, between the Shan and the Yung,
the porcelain atoms shivering at his touch,
ah, lighter than the emperor's breath, drinking rice wine from the bowl,
daintier than the eunuch pouring wine.

I came as quickly as I could
but already the fox had left the Industrial Revolution behind,
his eye has swept the age of atoms,
the Taj Mahal within the molecule.

The fox is in the fossils and the folios, I cry.
The fox is in Photography and the Folk Studies Department.
The fox is in the flux of the foyer,
the fox is in the flock,
the fox is in the flock.

Now the fox sniffs at the dodo
and at the door of Celtic orthography.
The grave-goods, the chariots, the gods of darkness,
he has made their acquaintance on previous occasions.

There, beneath the leatherbacked turtle he goes,
the turtle black as an oildrum,
under the skeleton of the whale he skedaddles,
the whalebone silver as bubblewrap.

Through the light of Provence moves the fox, through
the Ordovician era and the Sumerian summer,
greyblue the blush on him, this one who has seen so much,
blood on the bristles of his mouth,
and on his suit of iron filings the air fans like silk.

Through the Cubists and the Surrealists
this fox shimmies surreptitiously,

past the artist who has sawn himself in half
under the formaldehyde sky
goes this fox shiny as a silver
fax in his fox coat,
for at a foxtrot travels this fox
backwards and forwards in the museum.

Under the bells of *Brugmansia*
that lull the Ecuadoran botanists to sleep,
over the grey moss of Iceland
further and further goes this fox,
passing the lambs at the feet of Jesus,
through the tear in Dante's cloak.

How long have I legged it
after his legerdemain, this fox
in the labyrinth, this fox that never hurries
yet passes an age in a footfall, this fox
from the forest of the portrait gallery
to Engineering's cornfield sigh?

I will tell you this.
He is something to follow,
this red fellow.
This fox I foster –
he is the future.

No one else
has seen him yet.
But they are closing
the iron doors.

Madonna in Porthcawl

You'd never wonder:
or maybe you would.
Maybe you would look twice
if you knew her drug of choice.
Maybe you'd walk straight past
on your own saltwater and scarred weather pilgrimage.
Yes, maybe you'd wonder.
Maybe you would.

Because here she comes again,
strung out on the promenade;
a grandmother with limestone hair,
string-bag of catfood and sweet-
potato breasts aswing
beneath her stole.

She will not mow the lawn.
It turns into astrakhan.
Spiderwebs lean like unicycles
in corners of her porch.
But in November she placed
bubblewrap around the palm trees.
Wise too. I've seen snow
cover those winebottle trunks a good week.

But what brings her they ask what brings her
if it's not the wind that brings her or the fear or the fair or the tide
that brings her if it's not the terror that brings her what brings
her they ask if it's not last chances or the low prices that bring her
and not the writing in the red rock that brings her not the wind
the wound the times that bring her not the silence that brings her
they ask if it's not love that brings her and not the golf or the gulf
stream that brings her if it's not the house of clean needles or the
cuttle cathedrals that bring her what brings her
here

to live alone on the promontory
in her own microclimate
in the long grass and dog daisies,

because when it rains here it rains
all the stops on the harmonium.

But when it shines the anemones
are paparazzi crowding the pools.

And the wind?
The wind is landlord of this world,
posting dunes at the door like golden gangsters.

She must pay him in headscarves and appleblossom
the first Thursday in the month.

But how her tears fly.
Will she never learn our local trick
of looking with eyes closed?

At night I stand by the ruined wall to listen to her hymns.
She croons to the dead gods,
and to that special dead god in the twilight,
her voice through the palms almost a whisper now
accompanied by her lyre,
but maybe it was always a whisper, this grandmother
without grandchildren in her garden on the shore,
     that 40 watt in the attic
     hardly a film
     of moonlight.

     Still, never forget.
She has played to a cabaret
of vipers. Her voice has serenaded
a mortuary slab, her name been burned
upon a stormtrooper's neck.
Now, she smokes in a hammock,
considers the rain's blue balustrade
over Exmoor, plucks the sea
a lullaby until it falls asleep.

But mainly, she listens to the birds.
Because what she knows about birds
is worth knowing. For instance,
at night all larks are black and sing in Russian
but by noon become Asbury Park beachboys
auctioning their hearts.

Now, there she is again,
licking her 99 on the promenade
where the CCTV cameras are trained on the waves.
Never turn your back on an ocean is what we teach our children here,
    while John the Song tells her
how
      after one of our storms
      they used the pantomime broom
last held by a soapstar Cinderella
      to sweep a drift of purple starfish
      off the Grand Pavilion steps.

Listen:
surely that's her:
            the corncrake
the nightingale
          the buzzard with her bloody lip,
yes, that's her, that's her music
and all those songs irreducible.

Already she's learned our harmonies,
      writing a ballet
for statues: spending an hour
eavesdropping on the stonechat
clearing its throat, the scratchcard
choruses, the slang of grass. But I never said a word
when I met her beside the white bread.
Her trolley was filled with star-apples and sea-grapes
and she was wearing headphones.

I could have told her
    but I didn't.
    I could have told her then
it isn't all margaritas out on the driftwood deck.
    I could have told her that this
    is how we finish:
but I expect she knows already,
gazing at the sea, her telescope
scoping the sky between the black palms of Porthcawl:
    because forever now
she's out on the promontory with the rest of us,
    our huts on the shoreline,
    the tide in our shoes.

The Dolphin

It's not the shadow of a cloud or the shape of a shoal
so I ask what's out there –
as if the answer was concealed within myself.

Yes I ask myself what it might be
and after a while it is the swimmer that replies,
daring to show its deft muscle and delphic arc.

Next I start counting with my own heartbeat
and discover that every ten seconds this swimmer surfaces
like a bowsaw against the sea's green grain,
and that every ten seconds it leaps eastward
off the rocks of Gyrn y Locs towards the Irongate.

There are fathoms between us
but we are familiars. I am sure of that.
Because I have walked where it dives now
and I have swam where it is swimming
through the grey wall slow to fall in rubble,
through the white wall it has mined yet flies above.

And every ten seconds this dark dauphin
of the gwters and the gwlis and the grykes,
every ten seconds the Gulf Stream leopard
hurtles out of the salt thickets
and from where I stand on the cliff's dais
I can feel it coming, I can feel it coming,
so that the sea is changed and will never be the same.

Because here is the oracle of an ordinary tide –
something that cuts a crescent like the dark of the moon.
Then exultant in the air we both must breathe
is the polished ferrule of the dolphin's face.

The Cormorant

Don't think I don't know
who you are.
              Not even the soul
takes such a trajectory,
not even the cruise missile
on its flyby of El Rashid Street
flies so flat, homing in
under the sea's radar,
and what are you anyway
but a deathstar flicked by a
warrior-saint, a penny pitched
at the busker's guitar-case,
its blue silks opened
like a street autopsy?

So don't think I'm afraid to say
you bring the dusk with you
and all the limestone twilights
between Gwter Gyrn y Locs and Gwter y Cŵn,
dragging the west behind you
on fairground wings.

Because there's nothing else
that sounds like you and there's nothing else
that looks like you
and there's never been anything
that waits like you,
more patient than oil
in the departure lounges
under the sea-bed.

You're midnight's glove-puppet,
sentinel at the cavemouth,
something plumed and glassy-eyed
about you from the broom cupboard
of Porthcawl museum,
yet there you perch, on the capstan
by the quayside bodega
speaking the Arabic
of the corsairs, ventriloquist
of every cry that waits behind the dark.

Saltwater cockerel,
your oiled carcass floats
by the jetty. Is there no one who
will sweep away your blood's
black videotape?

But here you come again,
stealth-bomber out of the empty
quarter, trailing your own death
across the sky, in your heart
the ashes of American astronauts,
your forgiveness one black feather
taking a lifetime to drift
down from the stratosphere.

An Isotope, Dreaming

I saw them when I opened the caravan curtains:
hares boxing.
At dawn on the gravel
there they were, two jack hares standing up like firedogs,
or the scourgers who lassoed Christ's legs
and so tied themselves to him for ever,
the scourgers who are pistolwhipping the beardless Christ
there on the pulpit of St John's,
my two jack hares
beside this caravan.

Every evening I look west and say
redemption must be on its way.
It's in the red, it's in the reef, in the ray
as sunset swarms over Gower
and is gone.

The scientists were right
but so was RS.
            Resurrection
is in the reactor.
It's the atom that's reborn.
The soul perishes
but matter can never be destroyed.

One thing I've learned:
in the iron womb of Sellafield,
at the cubist monument of Trawsfynydd
and the accelerator tunnel at Berkeley
– that grey snake I once embraced in a jasmine garden –
the paradise particle will some day be revealed.

Now Swansea is burning again,
its sky the stained glass in the Brangwyn Hall.

The epicentre is Green Dragon Lane,
     and as the Guildhall
melts its limestone lifts
     like lingerie
while the football crowd becomes one man

and the prisoners run from the burning jail
        every cell a sun
until on Glamorgan Street
they're a guild of glass,
the roadrager, the childstalker, the lame houdini of the balance sheet:
        every man jack
        with every bone fired
        like a lightbulb's filament.

There is never only silence.
So listen to this
        and imagine
        inside the reactor
        the soft mutation
        of a soul.

There is different weather
in the atom now.

        We are all
        fuel rods –
        spent, eternal –
        radioactive gods
        enduring our deliriums –
        the half-life of angels
        that the world calls waste.

I have waited in my cave
for a billion years.

There will rise different cliffs
with new fossils
before they set me free.

Yet out of the terrible core I sprang –
warrior of a tribe that learned
to enrich language.

Now I am the isotope
dreaming.

Where they bury me
an idea starts to grow.

That's how a grave
becomes a temple.

I am the ghost that was given
a breastplate of lead.

But fools, standing guard,
their army did not see me pass.

Now I am the isotope
dreaming.

But what is the meaning of the half life?
In three places of this world I asked an answer.

On the first journey we were messing below
the mesa when I heard the geiger talk
like a black habanero rattling with seeds.

They called from the van:
                                          let's go, go back,
but the dust came with us down that dirt road
and the faster we went the more dust we saw,
a cloud of it, a
                              twister,
            the keels of its electrons
scraping my skin.

I was anointed by a devil
and sat still in the back.
What's the half life of the half life? I asked.

It's on your boots, they said.
                                          In your hair.
It's on the map that has brought us to this nameless place.
It's in my mouth, I said. It's on my skin.
It's in the earth under my nails and the fillings in my teeth.
It's in the water I drank and the mesquite I chewed.
And from now it's in my words and they will never let it out
because words are the green bones that we bend to make a child.

I was anointed by an angel
and sat still in the van.
What's the half life of a half life? I asked.

Outside her hogan
the child's horizon
was a black circle
on grey paper.
        Nothing else was allowed.
She followed the dust
back and forth;
it was in her hair
and on her skin,

a grey circle
on black paper:
and tapping its box
the scorpion's tail.
Now she is the isotope
dreaming.

There will be different cliffs
with new fossils
before they set her free.

        Nothing else is allowed
but a black circle
on grey paper
and a scorpion's tail
tapping its box.
        Back and forth
she follows the dust:
it's in her hair
and on her skin
this child who is the isotope
        dreaming.

In its bubblewrap my camera purrs:
it's the rock in which a fossil stirs.
        On the second journey
down the corridor I came and there was the cradle
and there were the twins. Look,
                                look
there at the twins, the doctor called
        and I saw
        the two halves
        of a black walnut.

The light's shrapnel lay between those hemispheres
but there was no balm for their wounds,
no barathea for those Basrans
born from the book of demons.

These were children never known before.
In their bones a ghost
was grinning, their blood
bankrupt. One's heart
was a forged passport, the other's
nerves the ruins of Nineveh.

We must learn these children's names, the doctor said,
who served the twins on their bleak bed
and had translated uranium's Koran
that was written into each chromosome.

But the information ministry had been looted by the mob,
the museum was smashed.
Smuggled out of paradise
the children were the first sounds heard
of the language that's to come.

Their arrival, the doctor whispered, was predicted.
One day I wandered down the boulevards
of Babylon. There was no one there.
I felt I must be the last inheritor,
and then on a wall above my head
I saw the children cut already into the clay.

    At the temple I stood
in an anteroom within an anteroom
and felt something strange within myself:
I became the tail that flickers without the lizard –

    back and forth and back and forth:
a kind of spell. My mind had ceased to work
and I was seeing with the soul.
All I remember is a mantis in a corner
like a creature blown from glass.

    The doctor touched my arm.
How small the Babylonians must have been, he said,

and held hostage by their own architecture.
That noon was full of nightmares:
because the griffins patrolled like gaolers of the citadel,
guarding the gods' entrance.

And slowly down that esplanade
came a marine from Omaha,
plainsman suspicious of the air,
a child in a cinder suit.
With his mask and cowl and silver epaulettes
he staggered like a moth shaken from a palm,
    a moth born to a bier
    in that bestiary.

And no, I don't feel sorry for your boys.
Let them anoint their blisters
with Exxon's frankincense,
wipe their arses with figs,
tip the bottles of bullets to their lips
and taste the pomegranate beer of old Shiraz.
We all sign up for something.

He held the sleeve of my filthy shirt and continued his story.
That night the patriots rose on golden wires
and I watched the Americans
chalk *grge washtn* on the tonsure of a tankshell.
        I listened to the earth
exhale and overheard the stealth
squadron already airborne
        already faint as the breath
of leverets asleep in their scrape
    one yard away from me
    on the wind-whitened nape
    of the dunes at Babylon.

    Such were the doctor's words:
an elegant man who had seen beyond himself.
And there were the twins he tended:
the welts of wings on their shoulders,
like two samaras that had spun to earth.
    But their cluster gave no clue.

It passes quickly. Passes on,
The gamma is the game we play at the gateway
the gam the ga the g in the gateway,
the atoms speaking in new tenses;
the word buds bearing different fruits.
    The half life of the half life.

    On the third journey
I stopped at the side of the road.
There were the trees. There were always trees:
the birch, the spruce, the pine upon its iron-coloured quilt.
    I stopped at the side of the road
to look in the mushroom sellers' baskets
and saw the crowns thrown in
        with the sceptres.

There was the pale boletus of Belarus
        yellow and white
        white and yellow
there were the Chernobyl mushrooms
        arching their madness
and the boletus that grows in the birchwoods of Belarus
and in the pinewoods of all its provinces.
    Theirs is the different weather
    in the atom now.

    Everyone I met
    cared for a garden
    and I gazed at what they grew:
mauves of a mournful Michaelmas
and beets to brew a borscht that would taste of frost and iron.

But everywhere was the boletus of Belarus –
in the graveyard, the schoolyard
and under the statue of Stalin
that they had hauled to the forest edge.

Two wrens had made a nest in his fist
and money spiders spun their moss
in a crease of Joseph Stalin's coat,
Uncle Joe whose proletarian
ferro-concrete pointed at the falling leaves
of a birch whose bark was a burnt missal,

black and silver, silver, black:
    an old newsreel;
    an old newsreel.
Uncle Joe rousted out of the city square
    to a grave under the trees.

    In the village
a woman came to her door.
She put up a hand to touch the wind,
the night wind that was passing through the leaves of her apple tree,
    the night wind
through the clusters of crab apples black in the moonlight,
    the last winter apples
    black in the moonlight
under the moon's microscope.
    An old newsreel:
    an old newsreel.

    Yes
I stopped at the side of the road
and there were the mushroom sellers
with their yarn spread over the yellow grass:
there were the mushroom sellers
who now are the isotopes
dreaming.

There will be different cliffs
with new fossils
before we set them free.

We split the rock
and they were waiting there.
We opened the atom's door
and who was it stood in greeting?

But you are welcome at last.
You are very welcome.
This is my mansion:
dust on the chandelier
and footprints leading to the garden.
Now evening's come and the children not yet home.

I will wait out the sun.
I will outwit the moon.

Around me the lights all die together
In Sŵn y Don, Bay View, the Esperance.
Even the Seagull Rooms have switched their televisions off.

And I sit in the caravan
and think of the hares;
the hares that dance at dawn,
the hares blue as the buckthorn.

My travels are over
but here are the trophies I brought home:
the ristra,
       the vodka,
              the rug from the suq.

    I was anointed
    by an angel
and sit here on the edge of the world –
    the waves on three sides.
Where the only road for is the only road against.

I will wait out the moon.
I will outwit the sun.

For there is never only silence.
Listen to me
    and imagine
    inside the reactor
    the soft mutation
    of a soul.

The g
      the gg
           the ga
           the gamma
      the game
the gamma
      ghosting towards
           the cell's gateway.

Such is the chariot racing through.
Such is the guest we all must greet.

And here on my peninsula I ask
where is the half moon and who is the half man
and what is the half life of the half life of the half life?

Yes you are very welcome.
I hope you guess my name.

    I who am the isotope
    dreaming.

An Opera in Baghdad

1

Here's a feather.
Made of fire.
Where's my father?
Made of fire.
All this fiddle.
Made of fire.
Fat and fifty.
Made of fire.
Fuddy duddy.
Made of fire.
Flesh alfresco.
Made of fire.

2

Saddam?
He ran
dressed as a beggar.
Dressed as a businessman.
Yes, Saddam Hussein, he ran away.

The Imperial Guard?
They ran too.
Those hundreds of the brave,
those hundreds of the true.
Yes, the Imperial Guard, they all ran away.

But the water boys there, every one of them stayed,
every one of them pissing themselves, every one afraid.
And they smoked and they swore and they gambled and they prayed.
The water boys there? Every one of them stayed.

They kept a canary down there in the gloom,
and it sang day and night in that terrible room,
as they tended the pumps that sent out the water
and they tried to forget the abominable slaughter.
Yes while the bird sang, like a shower of rain,
they forgot about Bush and Saddam Hussein.

You can call them the traitors, you can call them the mad,
but those were the best men there were in Baghdad.
They gave us the water when that's all we had.
Yes, they gave us the water, in the midst of defeat,
when the smart bombs were flying down Palestine Street.
Yes, they gave us the water when that's all we had.

3

Just bones.
High and dry.

So I sulk.
Just bones.

But the black stars
inside me now.

The black stars.
all inside.

Too soon. To the sun.
Too soon.

So blood boils. On a bed of nails.
Flesh fails.

The silver tongue.
The iron lung.

And I die.
High and dry.

4

The Tigris and the Thames. The Tigris and the Thames.
That's what I see, the Tigris and the Thames.
The Tigris green as kingfishers.
The Thames all sparrow brown.

5

I stood one night at Rotherhithe
and watched the river writhe,
the river writhe in Rotherhithe
and heard the barges creak and the drowned girls speak
in the Thames at Rotherhithe.

But as I made my way down Palestine Street
I smelled the wide Tigris,
the river smell that lifts the air
in a city such as this.
Then down on my head fell the barbarian sun
that knows no armistice.

6

Deep in the bunker at Amiriya
I learned another word for fear.
That's where I went to hear the truth.
That's where I found the baby's tooth.

       A milk tooth,
blue as a cinder. And it whispers:
coward, whose pain is it anyway?
Your cells are a blizzard,
your mind a ragbook, yet
I dream you into growth
luscious as papaya flesh
around my black seed.

Why this need to condemn what you find here?
You will carry me now
as a part of yourself.
In time I will feel your bones
gasp in their foundry,
and at night, you do not know,
but I will hear your blood
like a bench of silversmiths
pause at its work.
Then continue.

Forever now
I will ache in the skull
of the man who stooped in the shelter
of Amiriya to pick the tooth
of a child like a rice grain
from the ash.

7

The Tigris and the Thames. The Tigris and the Thames.
The Tigris black with blood.
The Thames all black with blood.

The Tigris filled with oil.
The Thames all filled with oil.
The Tigris and the Thames. The Tigris and the Thames.

The Tigris green as kingfishers.
The Thames all sparrow brown.
The Tigris and the Thames. The Tigris and the Thames.

8

As I made my way...
As I made my way down...

As I made my way down Palestine Street
I watched a funeral pass –
all the women waving lilac stems
around a coffin made of glass
and the face of the man who lay within
who had breathed a poison gas.

As I made my way down Palestine Street
I heard the call to prayer
and I stopped at the door of the golden mosque
to watch the faithful there
but there was blood on the walls and the muezzin's eyes
were wild with his despair.

As I made my way down Palestine Street
I met two blind beggars

And into their hands I pressed my hands
with a hundred black dinars;
and their salutes were those of the Imperial Guard
in the Mother of all Wars.

9

Here's a free man.
Made of fire.
Every feature.
Made of fire.
Forty footsteps.
Made of fire.
Full of feelings.
Made of fire.
Every fibre.
Made of fire.
Now a flower.
Made of fire.
All his fury.
Made of fire.
For a phantom.
Made of fire.
All this fear.
Made of fire.
Flesh alfresco.
Made of fire.

10

The Tigris runs through marshes where the herons are white.
The Thames runs through the marshes where the herons are grey.
The Tigris and the Thames. The Tigris and the Thames.

But I never drink the water. No, I never drink the water.
Of the Tigris. Of the Thames.
Of the Tigris. Of the Thames.

11

As I made my way…
As I made my way down
As I made my way down Palestine Street
I smelled the wide Tigris,
the river smell that lifts the air
in a city such as this;
but down on my head fell the barbarian sun
that knows no armistice.

As I made my way down Palestine Street
I saw a Cruise missile,
a slow and silver caravan
on its slow and silver mile,
and a beggar child turned up his face
and blessed it with a smile.

As I made my way down Palestine Street
under the yellow palms
I saw their branches hung with yellow dates
all sweeter than salaams,
and when that same child reached up to touch,
the fruit fell in his arms.

12

Find a fountain.
Made of fire.
Fill a funnel.
Made of fire.
Fluoro–carbon.
Made of fire.
Ferro–concrete
Made of fire.
Fuck the future.
Made of fire.
Find the fossils.
Made of fire.
All that's funny.
Made of fire.
Full of feasting.

Made of fire.
Here's a feather.
Made of fire.
Where's my father?
Made of fire.
All this fiddle.
Made of fire.
Fat and fifty.
Made of fire.
Fuddy duddy.
Made of fire.
In this furnace
of the fire.

13

But Radiohead said.
Radiohead said.
Creep, they said. Creep.
A creep crawls.

But I fly. I spy.
An arrow
To the atmosphere.

The bends. My friends.
I'm sent. Blood-bent.
Blood rends. The bends.

Creep, they said.
A creep crawls.
Dragging his chains.
But I fly. Too soon.
To the sun. With these pains.

A stone. A megaphone.
Blood bent I'm sent.

High and dry and high and dry.
I die.

With the black stars.
The black stars.

The bird in its cage sang an ancient maqam
of flowering fountains and rivers that ran,
of the rivers of Babylon, gentle to man.
Yes the bird in its cage sang an ancient maqam,
for those men in the pit who already seemed damned.
For the men who were doomed but continue to stand.

Yes they gave us the water when that's all we had
as it all went to hell on the streets of Baghdad.
They stayed at their posts in the fiery city,
maybe for love, or maybe for pity,
yes they stayed at their posts in all of that slaughter
because they were the men who worked with the water.

You can call them the traitors, you can call them the mad,
but those are the best men there were in Baghdad.
They gave us the water when that's all we had.
Yes, they gave us the water, in the midst of defeat,
when the smart bombs were flying down Palestine Street.
Yes, they gave us the water when that's all we had.

They kept a canary down there in the gloom,
and it sang day and night in that terrible room,
while they tended the pumps that sent out the water
and they tried to forget the abominable slaughter.
Yes while the bird sang, like a shower of rain
they forgot about Bush and Saddam Hussein.

King Driftwood meets the Viper

When I come upon her both of us are dreaming.
I am King Driftwood, pulling a spar,
    and she the caliph
on the ziggurat of her coils.

    A misfit like me,
I offer her my wrist to kiss.
    And she bends – a bow,
a billhook, in the sand.
Now look, there's my blood in the restharrow
as we rock together in light's centrifuge –
she in her pantherskin, I in ragged camouflage.

    How strangely she travels:
like a brass-linked chain
    someone is pulling through the grass.

Flat as a wrasse, as a ray, she passes,
a sand-sickle I'd say if I'd not seen
the spades, not diamonds, on her hide.

This neolithic is new to me,
    being fragments of a saga forged again.
    But the words inscrutable.

    One moment either way
I would have walked on.
    Instead I stare seven seconds
  at her Harlem shuffle
and wonder what the message is.

Her own whirlpool
  draws my eye
    into its eddy.
  Watching her, I lose
balance, might drown in her depths.

    Gold she is
  as the gorse needle
    hot in my heel.

The writing on her back
　　black broompods.

Hers an antique
jewellery. Old
woman's yellow
cairngorms. Broken
string of jet.

Hollow-beaked hawk, her venom
leaks into the sand.
　　　　　Where's the vine
to flay her on, the wall to stretch her skin?

This messenger moves
with poison in her purse.
The old news is new again
as she lifts herself like a lobe of mercury,
her mouth a dark searchlight.

　　　We bargained
and I lost.
　　　Here's the X
　　　where our paths crossed.
There's the rent in the world where she vanished.

I thought she was a stone.
Then she became a wheat stalk.
　　But always her throat was an iron orchid.

She's one I might in future understand;
yet the ghost in me knows
our tales will not be told,
each of us a grain in the gold moraine
the wind wears in the sand.

On Listening to Glenn Gould play Bach's Goldberg Variations

for my father

1

Here it comes
on its black sail
and surely nothing will be the same.
Out of the silence
in from the horizon
and nothing will be the same.

2

What can it be?
The dance of the viruses of course
under the theatre's glass.
Here's a waltz, a roundel, as they reproduce.
Meanwhile, up in the *paradiso*
the scientists have started their applause.

3

Listen to the notes
listen to the notes
as perfect as the pomegranates
and the plumage of the bee-eater
packed into the corporal's trunk.
What a world his expedition is bringing back.

4

I looked at the altar
and counted its glass dials
and its secret compartments and its golden pistons.
And I thought it was an engine,
an engine trembling there in the darkness.
And when I reached to touch I knew it was alive.

5

On a date-stone the beggar writes:

bells ring out —
a goat-train going past

all the dust in the desert
cannot make a man

must the emperor sing a requiem
for every child that dies?

What poem would he prick
upon the page of an emerald?

6

Sit with me
in the room where the mad
knit scarves no one will wear
and blankets that will not make a bed.
Sit with me and see every crimson thread
of the comforter that will bring no comfort.
Sit and listen to the needlesong
at the end of a life.

7

This is how
the atoms must behave
within the Great Mosque.
Only when the formalities are fulfilled
are they allowed to speak.

8

The scouts have not come back.
The captain is fevered.
    So it is the corporal
all skin-and-bone and ragged from Rangoon
    leads this advance,
the corporal who takes us
into the white light of the mind.

9

That is not the pianist
humming. That is the sound
of his mind
            ahrmm
                    ahrmm
            ahrnnmm
a still point as the world spins:
tape hiss of exultation.

10

Under the palm I dream of rubies
that turn to iron, that become a heap of stones.

Under the palm I dream of roasting meat
oozing its fat like a honeycomb.

Under the palm I dream of goatsmilk curd
in the desert of black sand.

Under the palm dreams the datepicker,
the datepicker with the withered hand.

The corporal steps back
amazed. There is a continent
behind the mist and a city beyond
every prediction. Look how
its citizens stream down to the shore –
cannibals with laptops and mobile phones.

You know what this proves?
That Einstein was correct.
    An object can exist
    in two places at once.
And that normal time's what the right hand
    leaves for dead.

Read me the score:
all the news from Leipzig,
all of this and more;
the black bread, the barbed wire,
the refugees in the refrigerator truck
writing their prayers on a screed of industrial ice.
All of this, I say.
All of this and more.

I stand in the office on Christmas Day
and there is the computers'
limestone, the English
language fossilised within.
And there – stonebreaker, mother of thousands –
the green perennial of the clock,
picked from the cliff edge.

15

Watch how the black sail vanishes
beyond the horizon ahead and the horizon behind.

So now we must wait at the child's bedside
and see her tossed akimbo, golden as the date heap.

Then this is where her sweetnesses start
as the sugars surge through her brain, her heart.

16

I sign my name
in the Poisons Book
and look, there I am,
deadlier than strychnine or the page that smells
of an Andalusian garden.
Then home I take the bottle
with its stopper of ground glass.
            Fools!
Forget your potions.
It was pride killed Socrates,
            old wise-guts
in his agony of self-love.

17

Who dies with me this morning?
        I say, who dies?
The cranefly's broken swastika,
the wasp encased in bubblewrap?
    Outside, the sparrows drop,
        the leaves let go.

18

A full moon
like a pheasant's eye
rises over the crest of the dune.
And here are the cuneiform
children at their somersaults:
the children pressed like letters
into the tablet of the sky.

19

The point of this
the point of it all
Sunday awaits
the point of this
the piano awaits
the point of this
the studio awaits
the point of this
God awaits
the point of this
Sony awaits
the point of it all

20

I touch the tiny Tigris child
and what is she
but a watermelon skin and a hank of wool?
As if the thief who comes to the treasury
takes away a single coin.

21

ahrmm
ahrmm
now it's 186,000
miles a second
but the pianist says
faster

we must go faster
if we want
              to leave ourselves
behind.

22

Silence.
There's not much happening in the atom today.
But upstairs in the dressing room
the electrons in furs and lipstick
totter round in their mothers' shoes.

23

You want to know what difference
words make? Ask the children
whispering under their hoods
in the occult tongue.
Ah, the little torturers!
It is breaktime now, a Mars, a Coke,
but after lunch, guess
who will be the first to be strapped to their iron bed?

24

    Big deal.
        We were created
when our universe was in collision
with another just like it.
        So today
              there is a small planet
where the oaktrees think and the people grow leaves.
And God is as red as granite
              and as cold.

25

Imagine, my darling, at the water's edge,
how beautiful you will become
when the waves are tucked under your chin
and the sea makes ready with her scissors and comb.

26

On the seventh day
God created migraine
and saw stars
and dreamed of sea serpents

the fossils hid themselves
behind his limestone beard
as electricity rode
nameless on the air

yet all the while
time was growing
like a tick on the blinded
lion of Kabul.

27

Her mother puts a towel over her face.
Too late my sweeties, my Adidas ball.

She is yellow as a reed in the wide Tigris.
Too late my pack of paracetamol.

They carry her away like a bushel of dates.
Too late my language, too late my love.

And save for themselves her pomegranates.
Too late the missile in the sky above.

Headphones, CDs. What shall I play?
    Desert silence
    the sea's farewell
    or my own heart's music
    – drum 'n' bass –
my own blood beating
like the fairground at the edge of town.

The dictator waits in the desert.
        For five thousand years that man of dust
        waits in the desert
        where once he wrote the future
        with his vermilion fingernail
and the sons of the astronomers
rolled their dice under Babel's hill.

The dictator waits in the desert,
        for five thousand years that man of dust
        waits in the desert
        where now he reads the future
in his book of mud, his cyanide pill.

    I was the hare
but my own life crept past me
under its grey shell.
What's for me now but
The Rough Guide to Sleep
and an attic with no lock in a seaside hotel?

Only my best clothes will do –
I'm a guest you see, a guest
at the mystical wedding of Saint Catherine.
How light she has become,
so light you might think she could float away;
but more beautiful than ever.
For here she is, the bride who steps
down the atom's glittering nave.

On the radio telescope, stars hiss
and planets whisper.
Or is that the corporal
   somewhere beyond all this,
his morse a music in the midnight air?

Why did I never tell him the war is over?
Now all I can do
is sing,
       sing
to show him
        despite everything
I was faithful too.

The Hourglass

Biding my time.
                Biding my time...

Third lesson in the high school and I look up suddenly.
I have taught in this room for thirty years
and told children about coastal erosion
and how there is order in the universe.

But I am growing old in their service
while my classes remain young.
Forty, fifty, but the girls
always seventeen. And the boys twelve.

      Hottest Day Ever
says the *Manchester Evening News*.
      I close my eyes and think:
tomorrow is Thursday. I will not come in...
      I will never come in again.

Now, what's that?

      That sound?
         It's sand
in its auditorium
         applauding itself.

Because sand can do anything.
Yes sand can do anything
but sleep.

The land slips by.
              Lordy, how the land slips by.
Cliffs on castors and rocks unriveted from immemorial plinths,
            scenery teetering
as on some vaudeville stage.

         Sand,
you were Nebuchadnezzar once,
The Lords of Dahomey. Now, sleeping off the latest sesh
         which you will not recall

a street cleaner rousts you with his broom
in the gutter behind the Buccaneer.

Yes, there lies sand,
a haemophiliac boy
with highlights in his hair.

Sand,
you were the special one.
You took the Sphinx to fifteen rounds,
out-manoeuvred Ozymandius from the first.
More grains in you than words in Wikipedia.
Ah, virgin under the veil,
you are the necromancer
writing backwards in an upside-down book,
a magpie that drops a golden quoit into the latrine.
That's you, sand.

So has sand
sinned? That shifty gait, such wry
restlessness. A guilty conscience,
I suspect.

When the beach travelled past at twenty-five miles per hour,
knee-high, white and whispering, going east,
I thought it a sail on some argosy.
Yet how strange to think.
I live in a country that is leaving me behind.

And yet, such energy,
you know what I mean?
I need, I want
sand's amphetamine.

Suddenly the sky
purple as toothwort.
Deadbolts drawn
but sand already in the freezer,
the safe behind the portrait of the Laughing Cavalier.
Ah, it's your nature sand:
fox and scorpion learned their ethics from you,
your glacier approaches like the Rawalpindi Express,
a simoom grinding its gears.

Yes, I thought, sand
is a library: sand is
Prozac Nation, *Ecclesiastes*, *The Dream Diary of Teenage Tanya*.
But sand is also *Das Kapital*
with the punctuation taken away.

That heavy breathing on the phone?
It's sand, of course, bored with being alone.

I had dialled the sand chat line.
What a mistake. Now the calls come
every night. Every day the texts, the threats.
Sand sold my number
to the sea. I'm thinking of coming round,
says a voice. Because I know
where you live.

How sand gloats.
Since carbon copped for us
we sulk for silicon.

At Kenfig the fog
fell in a golden
Götterdämmerung. The swan, the sanderlings,
the conger cold as cistern-iron?
The famished sand filched that feast.
And the poets who practised there left nameless;
welldrivers, grapegrowers, wolfwatchers likewise.
If any escaped
they are unrecorded. Only the castle sometimes
is mistaken in the mist.
How drunk was that watchman
he missed the dune at the door?

A simple question. Or so I thought.
Who is the saint of sand? I asked.
But sand only stared at me, thin and unsunned.
You need a holiday, said sand at last. I know just the place.

How far, I asked of sand.
How far? As far as
the Sahara's final finial.
That's how far.

On Olympus we passed
the poets weeping
into their websites.
We wanted fame, they cried.
But not for this. Not this.

    Every winter at Punta Ala
when the villas are shut up and the restaurants closed
sand would stride up the beach and into the *pineta*.
      This time I was sand's companion
and we moved farther than ever before
and came upon a field of sunflowers:
a thousand sunflowers black in the moonlight,
ten thousand sunflowers in their ruin,
      each face a black zodiac,
an army of sunflowers leaning on their spears,
      some spell upon them,
an enchanter's curse or a draught from a poisoned well.

A child was singing in that midnight
and we stopped to listen to her Etruscan lullaby.
Behind us stood the lighthouses of Napoleon's island,
      on and off. On, off:
      tall as sunflowers, I thought.
      And then sand laughed.
Because what is buried must be revealed
      and nothing stays a secret long.
Or so said sand of that dark syndicate.

    Moab might be Lot's grandson and massive ordnance air blast but tonight it's the mother of all burgers. Yet soon that neon charcuterie is left behind as we climb to Chapel Road and in the Datsun start to crawl round the haçienda.

    Headlamps off, we're a black car in unpolluted darkness. The house too is unlit. The gates are closed and there's no guard.

    But then, who is that? Up there in the tower? A figure is gazing, skywards of course, ever skyward, the telescope barrel pointing north east. So I look with it.

    Hey, where did these come from? Such raw constellations: the Cactus, the Cadillac, the Habanero. I've never seen them before.

    Got to be Cage himself, hisses sand. Built the house specially, didn't he? For the sky. The empty sky.

So while Nicolas Cage is scoping the sky we're stalking the
stars. Yes, Nick Cage. I think of him in *Leaving Las Vegas*,
tipping that quart into himself like it was mother's milk. As if
he was filled with ashes and he opened his mouth to a cloud-
burst. Call it irrigation. As if he was filled with sand.

Okay, maybe in reality he's not so great. Those sad tattoos?
But you have to have a model, see. A role model. And Nicolas
Cage might be mine. Because Cage built an observatory. And
now he's up there looking at all this; the fireflies, the UFOs, the
shakedown of meteors over the desert.

I can picture that glass he brandishes. Black lens with a rain-
water meniscus set in a gold bezel. So I'm here too, sneaking
with sand round his villa in the piñon pine and prickly pear, an
audience outside his theatre. Because where else should we be,
tell me that, when rising from the rimrock is this midnight moss
of mezcal-coloured stars?

      But so far, said sand,
everything has been displacement activity.
There are great things to which I aspire.
One day they will be revealed to me.

Here is a clue.
    How the arboreal
      bores me. If a leaf's first life
is grace then fast falls fire and grief.
    The olive and the baobab
are bones under my battering ram.
Ahead I smell a country of oaks
and orchards, that rumour of silence
      amidst skeletons of the spruce.

      Remember, I was in Eden too,
said sand. The snake squeezed over me
and I felt it as I feel children's fingers writing their names.
That serpent slept lidless in a cave while I kept guard
      and whispered to it.
                    If only
you knew, I told it,
              my every grain is red
              as a pomegranate.

Okay.
      I confess.

I thought sand a lost cause.
                No visa,
            no English,
          no hope.
But there it was on the slipway,
the sudden sand in sodden silks.
How could we send it back?
(Some tried poking it with a stick).

              Here are the signs
              of catastrophe:
            magpies at their pillage;
            burdock dark in the barley;
soon, a pittering, a pattering upon that green leather
polished for a century by every parliamentary arse.
Next, the Prime Minister rubbing something from his eye.
          It is with regret, he says. So much regret…

You might drown in a drop
I heard sand explain,
not thinking I
could be crushed by a grain.

And always towards:
that's how sand moves, always
towards and never away.
Never back, even in retreat.
Even in retreat
it's always towards.

Yes, I thought. It came in a flash.
What sand teaches
is that there's no oblivion.

            So consider sand,
              that sorcerer full of secrets.
What shape should sand assume?
A girl in beads, braids and barrettes?
Sumo, sapsucker, the old Sumerian writing the law?
But I saw sand acting up in Arcadia's aisles,
Lou Reed's 'Perfect Day' on someone's mobile
and all the jackpot silver still untouched.

The second time I went officially with sand
we passed through the checkpoint at Lukeville.
Two miles into the desert I watched a soldier pull
a Mexican boy off the back axle under a bus.
        An illegal, see. One of the legions of La Lucha.
        And all following the north star
        above *El Camino del Diablo*,
        past the Barry Goldwater Airforce Base.

I looked into the eyes of that soldier and he was twenty, max.
Biding his time. Biding his time.
But in those eyes I saw the prehistoric ash
and glimmering fulgurite of every desert place.
He was a sand man, see. Oh he was one of us.

Of the twenty-six ahead, counted sand,
fourteen are already dead, seven of thirst, seven from sunstroke.
Their tongues are black as the pumice stone.
One man, seeking shade, has pushed his head
into the badlands crust and his brains have boiled.
The remaining twelve are walking north. Slowly.
    Will they reach the border, I asked?
Bah to borders, said sand. Borders are dreams.
Those lines in the sand were drawn by rattlesnakes.

        But ugh,
      the ergs,
the eskers,
      the sinks,
the cirques,
       the barrens,
              the barchans.
On the crest I needed goggles
as if watching an eclipse,
my boots worn white as cuttlebone
and sand in its cylinders twisting through the sky.

Here we are at last, said sand.
This is *El Gran Desierto del Altar*
where no man has ever set foot.
Even Cortez turned away, Cortez
the killer and his iron army.
And here you stand, pilgrim

And on that crest I thought of Mars
because when sand rubs
      a cinder
it reveals
      a ruby.

But it was a wind from Morocco
put the iron in the face of the sandhills moon,
    so low down
    I looked into it
climbing the north-facing dune,
so low down I looked directly into it
and felt that I could touch the blood bruise on the sky –
that moon the sand had smoked redder than chilli oil.

After that we rested, sand and I,
cool in the corals of Cog
y Brain, a parish that had prospered
under sand's perpetual
curacy, commote of vipers' milk,
every twmpath of Tir y Hwndrwd
a honeyed tomb, a terraced vault.

From there we surveyed the world.
    Sometimes I can be good, said sand.
At Oxyrynchus I blew away from the town
and that is how they discovered the Iliad on a thousand papyri.
    Not all the words, you understand,
that was a poem I needed to rewrite.
But I watched the professors dig for those pages
and wondered when they might realise
    that sand is the true epic.
 Because sand is not gossip
      but a gospel
      announcing itself.

      It was there sand told me
its torments. The time it was locked
      in a Palaeolithic vice
and mocked by the scum of the earth;
    when it was confined
    to the empty quarter
    then banished in shame

to Badiet Esh Sham,
how it must career around the caravans, blind
and unbidden, every door against it:
incontinent sand, the earth's orphan.

Ah, stop whining, sand, I say.
        Take your Ritalin.
        And that's when I look up.

There is ash in my hair, silver in my teeth.
        The children are observing me,
        each with a lunar face;
        and every child an altar, an anvil
        and every face my own deathmask.

Yes there is my class
  waving their hands with answers
    I can never know.
      Or are they saying goodbye
    as they watch me pass
  grain after grain
into the hourglass?

La Otra Orilla

1 Tickertape

For days
I never opened my mouth,
afraid of the stranger who would speak with my voice
and the thief who lived under my tongue.

Learning the language
was like eating its seafood
– *chipirones*, *pulpitos* –
when Gotan my friend, took me to the café
and every word was squidgy as a mussel
under its blue door.

Verbs
were lemon-edged, like samphire;
conjunctions beckoned with their department-store glass:
how I loitered there.

Then, a breakthrough.
Ice-cream at the *kiosko*,
and a glass of Malbec with Gotan
in a bar made of corrugated iron painted pink;
and that afternoon, waiting for the lights to change on Rivadavia,
I looked up and the sky was full of words.

Immediately
all the bills of lading from La Boca
were blowing like the jacaranda petals around my feet,
and the special offers and the final demands
and the Vallejo stanzas and the bank statements
and Borges's foul copies of *El Aleph*
and every second chapter from *Kiss of the Spider Woman*,
all the molecules of books were adrift on the air.

Next came
the repossessions and the summonses,
the timetables from the language school where Gotan worked,
and soon the languages themselves from the sacristies
of paper, and the professors from the language school

throwing armfuls of idioms out of their office windows,
and the secretaries of the professors from the language school
photocopying their kisses and scattering them from the third storey.

Then the black-browed
subjunctive plummeted like a suicide
and with it the future-perfect, mauve as the magnolia,
and there was Menem's manifesto
and then the biographies of the disappeared
disappearing as the wind hurried them down the *avenidas*
to the sea that would greet them once again.

And with them fell
the love-songs that the student had written for the torturer
so he might serenade his sweetheart on his day off,
and behind them the *empanada* menus
and the words on the cigarette butts
and the bullets and the wine bottles and the toilet walls,
and there were the epitaphs traced from the tombstones
and the paint of the street names scraped off the street signs.

For days
I had not opened my mouth.
I let Gotan do the talking and instead
groaned like my father in his blue smock,
his left cheek fallen, his left arm deciduous, daunted
by the anarchy of his own tongue,
but now, here I was with the soldiers
and the corn-roasters on the Plaza de Mayo
as the words fell upon us in their tickertape blessings.

And in that *pampero* of paper
were words for the desperate and words for the newborn;
there was wealth for the *cartoneros* beyond every dream,
and the beggars around us were filling their trousers with passports
and telephone directories and death sentences,
and there was Gotan lying on the ground
with *La Nación* covering his face
and there I stood with arms outstretched
and the letter 'I' dissolving in my hand
    like a hailstone.

2 Teatro

Yes I am coming with golden Colon,
coming to Colonia,
coming with golden Colon
to Colonia across the sea.

      Weekends
I'd go with Gotan to the flea-markets.
There's nothing he loves better
than barter on those San Telmo Sundays
with pimps and astrologers and the admiral
in a uniform mottled like a mirror,
or the country kids come up from the farms
carrying sacks of sunflower seeds.

      Once I found
he'd bought an apparatus that gleamed
like a bordello of glow-worms.
It was an absinthe engine, he whispered,
all spouts and glasses, inlaid with silver
vermiculations. Baudelaire, he said,
is my hero, after DJ Shadow and mon cher
Che. Maybe John Coltrane.
And this absintheizer is the crucible
where the senses are rationally,
which means with a recipe, deranged.
Then Gotan grinned like a thief.

We'd seen La Boca's ships scabbed by the sea,
the hulls molten with rust, its lava at their sterns and bows,
and all La Boca's colours in the oil painting
I carried, a few pesos she said, so I paid the artist,
that girl with burgundy about her eyes and vermilion upon her toenails,
      and carried La Boca through La Boca,
that picture a bargain said Gotan, I am an artist myself you know,
but in soundscapes, recording La Plata's tides,
      my tapeloops in all the clubs,
      the nightclub children in each other's arms
      watching dawn break to my birdsong,
      my remix of the revolution

with CNN news
cut to confetti.

One night we met Gotan
outside an apartment block
where the electricity was turned off
and we could see children's candleshadows
as they went to bed, families ghosting
through winelight.

Downtown,
Gotan knew the way
and I followed him upstairs to a bar
with a coffee machine so dinted and stained
it might have been some Toledo cuirass
targeted by untold Querandi stones,
and we took our café by the glass
under Teatro Libre's black curtain
and never forget
he said
never forget
the burning palm trees of a bankrupt republic
and that a chief of police will listen forever
to the empire's pornographic sigh.

But absinthe, Gotan breathed,
is how the soul communicates.
Its wormwood parables are untold by the tongue.
Drink and you'll discover dreams in the dirt under your fingernails.
Our life must be served in prism sentences.
Abstinence
will be my nemesis.
It's delirium that drives.

Behind the curtain lay a darkness so thick
I could not see my hand
but there was Gotan's hand upon my back
and we sat on school benches
and waited until something
came out of the blackness –
an owl's face
or a woman in owl's feathers –
a woman with a belly white as a garlic

bulb and grinning with her mouth
on fire in an owl's head-dress –
grinning I saw, in front of the drapes
that blacked out even the starlight of my skin.

Hardly the Paradiso, whispered Gotan,
as the torturers explored
pain's tautology. But still
the best seats in the house.

After the show we went for a beer –
the cool Quilmes on our tabletop –
and we drank like men shackled to our cups
until Gotan sat back and sang his nursery rhyme

Yes I am coming with golden Colon,
coming to Colonia,
coming with golden Colon
to Colonia across the sea.

And when I wake I will rub
the sleep from my ears
in the house of harpsichords.

    But what waited in that darkness?
The regime's rapeocracy.
After the women died
they raped the children
and after the children
they raped the men
and then they raped the dogs
after the men died
before they raped the mossgowned
sloth hung like an angel
in metropolitan amnesia.
And after the women had died
and the children died
they planted rape in this country
and the rapeflower grows in the mountains still
and in the streets. It is pale
      and light
          as lithium,
a herb they say that's medicine

for memory and white as a bride's veil
that drags across the desert dusk
until caught on a cactus.

The next day
I saw Gotan and his girl
with their kettledrums
outside the Casa Rosada;
then later on in all La Boca's bars
kissing the teargas out of each other's eyes.
Haven't we cried enough, the girl asked,
aren't there enough tears in this world?
Damn them, damn them, she waved,
as if the generals stooped about them now like vultures in gold braid.

Yes, think of Colonia,
where cats curl up on cannonballs
and breakfast lasts all day
until sleep, il generalissimo,
drafts you to a dream.

And when I wake I will wake
where I always wake
in the house of harpsichords.

The answer, said Gotan, is anarchy.
That's why I will never buy an apartment in Puerto Madryn
or watch Tom Cruise at the multiplex
or accept a PIN number from HSBC.
        As to the bankers,
        stuff their hearts with pepper
        and their bellies with broken glass.
        Freeze them in prisons of Patagonian ice.
.
And soon he was whistling the march to the scaffold
that Berlioz wrote, and laughing like
Berlioz's absinthe-coloured demons
as if they were dancing out of the metro
and dragging the souls of soldiers and blackgloved
police and sneaks and senators and helicopter
pilots, of pimps, of *putas* and poets,
of pacifiers and expurgating editors,
of the fat, the fascistic, the freighted with lies,

the disinformers, the unmakers, the antipriests
and antiteachers, the lawyers
bound like *burros* to each other by their Jaeger ties,
the journalists who had never interrogated themselves,
dragging them through the turnstile
past the painted aborigines
who once walked naked on the glaciers,
past the prehistoric bones of flightless birds,
past conquistadors who watched from their battlements
immortal in the twilight armour of armadillos:
      to the train to hell or Ushuaia,
      whichever station comes first.

3 Las Cataratas

    It is time to leave
but Gotan will not let us
go. One last adventure, he pleads,
to make sense of everything.

Forgetting the city we take the Marco Polo north
and travel all night and the only sign of human life
is firelight struck in oil drums
and bodies prone around each dying blaze.

But what arrives with the dark
is lightning. Gotan says he is a connoisseur
of lightning; it is masque and muse
to him, an electric mass.
Tonight its incendiaries race out of a sky
the colour of a tattooist's inks.

My seat is next to the coffee machine.
The Marco Polo coffee is black and hot and so sweet
I shiver at the first taste, trembling
with the saccharine rush. But now I hold my cup
in both hands as if refusing to let go
while the land dries out, the forests change,
the pampas stars burn huge and indecipherable
and gauchos ride with us a moment
out of the mist. And I hear Gotan
singing in his sleep

Iguaçu night
Iguaçu night
Pumas black as pumice
In the Iguaçu night.

Soon we are the only ones left.
As we alight the bus is driven away.
Or perhaps it simply disappears.

Over there, says Gotan, and we have to follow.
At last, he says. Here are *las cataratas*.
At our feet a pit opens.
Inside the pit a rainbow writhes.
Here there is sky where there should be earth.
Here there are birds where they might be fish.

   Only swifts invade
   this void but
   Gotan says the pit
   is not for us.

Who comes with us? we call.
No one, says Gotan. We are the last
   but for those toucans –
   those toucans with their terrible beaks,
   their stone language;
   those toucans with telephones in their mouths –
   those toucans can too.

And Gotan sings to us

   Rainforest night
   rainforest night
   pumas black as pumice
   in the rainforest night.

At our feet
the pit of white light
where we will be unearthed.

      We can go no further –
no further than the ledge where the swifts lodge
in their black moss, mollusc-birds with wings

sharp as mosque-moons, the last creatures
of all before the world ends
and the rainbow makes a bridge
through the abyss,
a bridge that we must
trust.

You must understand, says Gotan, this is the only way.
Behind us is the *tigre* that took the park ranger's son.
Its eyes are *aguardiente*, each paw a lily pad.

There is no bridge, we tell him.
Che baludo, don't leave us on the edge of nothing.
    At our feet
    a pit of white light
    where we will be unearthed.

Jump, says Gotan. Behind us is the *tigre*
that murdered Maradona's mother. One last adventure,
my friends, think of all we have been through together:
    think of the toucans –
    those toucans with their terrible beaks,
    their stone language;
    those toucans with telephones in their mouths.
    The *tigre* took those toucans too.

At our feet the pit opens;
inside the pit a rainbow writhes.
It is more than time, says Gotan.
The clocks have started to go backwards.
We must join *los desaparecidos*
and then this last adventure will make sense of everything.
Behind us is the *tigre* the Guarani trapped
that Evita might wrap her shoulders in its silks.
To understand our history we must cross the bridge.

So I take the step.
I take the step and the coffee
is black and hot and so sweet I tremble as I taste.
And there is Gotan, his head against my head,
whispering in his sleep

Iguaçu night
Iguaçu night
pumas black as pumice
in the Iguaçu night.

And there are the herds and there the stars' junta,
for still there are more stars than steers,
and as we gaze together at the roots of the day
the meniscus of the new moon
is pale as a palmito
above us this night, this noon
where we must be unearthed.

King Driftwood meets the Vagabond Surf

There he is now. In his salty boots, a fisherman's cagoule. Yes here he comes now. Muttering that song, always that song. But don't look at him. No, don't look. You have to glance away. Because he'll catch your eye. And if he catches your eye he'll meet your mind.

All right, he's gone. But he'll be back, drifting down the esplanade. Yes, he'll be back, you can count on that, a beachcomber like him never goes far. But he's older looking now, his face an oyster shell, though mother-of-pearl his laughter.

Because he keeps an inventory of it all, and what he finds he never forgets. I've watched him writing, copying it into his book of tides. Such laborious letters. Semi-literate at best, I'd say. Bad parenting, bound to be. Rock pool genes. Or genius. So what he keeps and why he keeps it are difficult to understand. Every wave a wafer, every watery waif. Too much rhyme and not enough reason, but when was he ever reasonable?

Anyway, it's all packed into that supermarket trolley of his. Full of the sea's distemper. So here's some of it. A list, I suppose, like a Tesco receipt but without cashback. Doesn't make sense but he's too old for making sense.

Tampons, tempests, a turbot's tumours. A dogfish gutted by gulls on Gwter y Cŵn. High tide jellyfish from the night club steps. Sea lace, whipweed, bladderwrack fat as figs. Chitons like quillets in the karst. The terrible tributyls. Then pantyliners, gas cylinders, Japanese aerosols. Polystyrene, a submarine, a brigantine. Cadmium, copper, Ambre Solaire factor forty. Violet anemone breathing. Breathing. A Venetian astrolabe, a Fulton Street fish market icebox, a lifebelt from Miami Beach in Port Talbot.

He sees it all, taking what he needs, this pisspoor Poseidon who picks through the foam and lords it over the laminarian world. Shelley's septum like a crabshell hangs about his neck, the cabin notebooks of Hart Crane, Alphonsina Storni's left slipper. And an isthmus too. And an island. With shoals, with shallows, with shad. A poppy from Sker scree, yes a yellow horned poppy from the skerry. Seventeen abortions out of the storm sewer. And lug. And laver. And more lug and more laver and lavender, more sea lavender mauve as lovehearts.

Then there's cuttle, there's cockles, there's scurvygrass. Sometimes a dolphin, skewbald, stinking. Sometimes a sunfish. Once a basking shark polished like a piano.

And sand of course. There's always sand. And with sand comes sand's syndrome. It's called Attention Deficiency Syndrome. So sand isn't sent. Sand sends itself, a fanfare in the funfair, its veil on the wave, its vowel in the wind.

And the solitudes, the disappearing solitudes. He has those too, if you require them. And silence. The debacle of silence. The atrocity of silence some would call it who might have overheard his incantations. Then lingered to count the hairs in his nostrils.

He's mad, I'd say. He has to be mad to live like this. Do you know what they call him? The Vagabond Surf. Yes that's what they call him. But look away now. He's coming back.

St John's Sunflowers

Your Royal Highnesses?
    Mr President?
       Mr Prime Minister?
The sunflowers will see you now.

Safe in their silos sleep the sunflowers.
No warhead gleamed so brightly.

I take the communion of sunflowers
 – the green loaf, the black wine –
and behind me follows the fox, the firefly
and the Phantom, its missiles
filled with sunflower seeds.
    Such are the faithful.

The sunflowers are moving:
the sunflowers are moving
but they cannot escape their staves.
Each is chained to the rock
    like a rottweiler.

    In the darkness
I listen to the sunflowers
      breathe
and their faces are malachite with the moon upon them,
    the ore magnetic within.

It is as if the blacksmiths of Nottage forge
had poured them from a ladle.
I know another season soon follows the sunflowers
but still their plasma refuses to cool.

Drowsy, dogdayed,
the salt air turns their copper faces green.
How many channels can they receive?

Hasten the host.
We are believers
we are all believers
in a religion of sunflowers

as their winged children chant
in a church of sulphur
and iron becomes
iridium.

Yellow,
it does not yield,
this sunflower whose pollen
is promethium,
whose neck
carries the nervous system of flame.

The tallest sunflower wins a prize
but so do the weirdest vegetable and the longest bean.
Democracy's a demon sent to drive us mad.

When the electricity goes off
and the electricity goes off so often these days
I sit under the sunflowers
and read *Les Fleurs du Mal.*
Yes, yes, it's as the poet says:
with any gutrot
mindache
worldwarp
we must make ourselves worse to get better.

Yesterday my daughter pressed a seed into a pot.
Now here's an angel she sends me, dreaming already
upon a pillow of pincushions.

Wearing dark glasses I look at the sunflowers
whose faces are nylon backpacks stuffed with Latin nouns.

Such a feast under the microscope
as the scientists savour the atom's
attar. In Babylon the sunflowers
are yellow as uranium.
Heavy the harvest home.

Evenings, the sunflowers summon us.
They are a bench of judges in black caps.
Guilty guilty guilty guilty guilty.

When comedians, criminals and artichokes
in the VIP enclosure
are shickered on champagne
only the sunflowers are not superfluous.

Stop a moment to look at the sunflowers
                under their rind of rain.
What might we say to them?
Fresh-faced as Jesuits
                they must know another way.

The men who grow sunflowers are serious men.
They groan in the grass, the sky
the colour of their trouser pockets
as their sins sway golden before them.

But the fire falls out of them,
these waifs bound in brass.
        Look at them die –
their soul-smoke white as wire.

Their music is too sad for us.
        There's thunder all afternoon,
then beneath the altar at St John's
the sacrificial sunflowers are laid down,
the organist smiling like an axe.

        Five times a day,
at the shrine of Ali, below Babel,
the soles of the worshippers' feet
grow radiant as sunflowers
        beyond the hill of shoes.

Now here comes the gravedigger
whistling. We'll leave the grammar to him
and the spelling to the gardener
and wait for the sunflowers to ferment the words
themselves, hot and holy as summer beer.

They cut open the St John's sunflowers
and saw there was nothing to be done.
But the crowd demands the heads, the hearts,
as the crowd demands the medicines and the missiles
that will make us brave.

So we lay them down.
Such a forest they made.
We lay their yellow down
in the sump of the sun.
We lay them down
in the heap of dark and glittering things
that we call home.

Eavesdropping

4 a.m.
and the swifts
over the house in the disappearing
dark, the swifts open-mouthed, ten,
twenty of them, thirty swifts now
and in every open-mouthed swift I picture
a heart the size of a hawthorn berry,
blood red to bursting those swift hearts,
thirty hearts in thirty swifts
over the house this morning where I stand
naked at the window, listening to my own heart –
perhaps the closest I will get to prayer –
and eavesdropping on the silence of the morning
where every swift is a black new moon upon the black mosque of the air.

The Castaway

Sleepless
I keep sleep in my pocket,
insomnia a sea-urchin language
and the nights strung together dried like chillies,
the red, the black, the ceaseless, the unbearable,
the darkness of chilli wombs rattling with stars.

But every night
a whale in the bay
spits at the moon.
Though it does not exist
how quickly I put my serenade together
for our low-tide rendezvous.

Look at me, I say to the no one there.
One day these bones will be silver in the sea holly.
But today I darken, I darken,
my skin a caste-marked congregation in a chancel of salt.

The town astronomers
are camped upon the dune
measuring Mars as it rides over Somerset.
Maybe I should throw my spear at them
or serve rainwater in an oystershell.

Such a current.
I call it *El Generalissimo* –
for only the current can say
where the disappeared people have gone.

I fear lightning, jellyfish, the uncomprehending mind, call
centres, ticks, the data protection act, search parties, autopsy, sand-
fleas, journalism, tourists, tiger sharks, whirlpools, translation,
the storm ten miles offshore whose ziggurat is built from one
billion tons of rain, rain bricks, imperial staterooms of rain with
rain's imperial family now waving from their balcony overhead.

It was for this I bartered
my breath? But at dawn a footprint,
and in twilight a crab army

circumnavigates the camp.
　　Meanwhile I'm refining
my religion.
　　　　　To hell
with the sutras of sand:
every day that gospel changes.
My latest god is the driftwood god and I am driftwood's dizziest disciple.
See his altars with their pilot lights ablaze upon the tide.

My mermaid I made of marram
the storm stole, she lifted, green
grass angel, over the point,
not an outline left of her or a
trace of the garden I trod her in the chalk,
and after weeks waiting not a word to her
guardian of the one who ascended
without sin or sign, my
wife from the midden,
my wife in mid
air.

The cormorant is always
black. But not blacker
than the blacknesses the ocean will become:
even the cormorant's eye will be black that an hour ago
was the Peruvian gold of Mars as it scorched the sky.

　　Destiny, they say,
is all: our pre-natal
navigation. So the poet sets out
over the shelves of Spezia
and there's my mother madcap on the shore
sewing his shipwreck into a shroud.

　　Every day
the sea smells stronger on my skin.
At last I am utterly clean,
anointed with crowfeathers, battery
acid, the fair's cinnamon
doughnuts, sulphur in the dune-rift
and fire from the fumeroles in the seabed,
until my blood rings against salt's armour.

So, which sea tonight?
The waif?
   The wolf?
Yes.

Traeth yr Afon low tide:
 the beach a looted exchequer:
 barbarians streaming away.
 I start again.

Now the current is dark and all its candles
pinched, its voices vanished like so many
voices that failed at midnight, and the sea's library
in darkness, in its greatest darkness, every book of it
and every page fused to blackness, every word and signature
translated into the language of the dark.

 Patience he played
 and patience he showed.
I'll show him patience, that no one there.
Here's the wayfarer tree upon the shore –
as if my father had left his diamonds and spades
 all over the beach.

  August
I'm spending under a hunter's moon.
 Tides come in like brickdust,
and all the sprockled moths mad in the wall rocket.
 Sometimes I lie on the seabed
 to look at the sun.
And sometimes I think drowning's
 a white door
 behind a white
 door where a fire
 burns on a dark
  isthmus.

First
there is an island
 then
there is no island
 then
there is.

                Or:
a sleeper in the ocean
who rises and
                shakes himself
out of his limestone trance
                every eleven hours.

    In my own dream
            I was a glass
statue on the sand with the sea
surreptitious behind the mist.
            And in my glass belly
beat the last
            Adonis of the dunes,
the last thought I would ever have,
            the last creature I could dare to be.
            I stood,
a statue on a shell-dust plinth,
the invisible ocean's foam
to my femurs and the butterfly
tormented in the glass web
            of my veins.

    They told me not to swim
at night, but the cormorant is a great cartographer
and I follow the compass in his heart.
            Yet who knows these roads like me?
I put out my hand and the darkness pulls me in
and I join the army of the invisibles
whose breath is black, whose blood is black
and whose wine is the colour of the waters under the waters.
            They are waiting for me
            in the amnesiac room:
they are waiting for me to open my black mouth
and tell them all I have learned of the collision of midnights,
of the sea's unseen catastrophes.

    My sentry
is the mullein in its greatcoat.
And strange – the sea going out and going
out and going beyond me somehow,
so in place of the garden where I floated

– nose and ears stoppered by the wave's pollen –
lie the bureaucracies of mud
    and a conger family
    fletched like school railings.

Television people come to ask
what I eat. Only oysters
oiled with samphire, I say:
or fennel's green shuttlecocks;
maybe kedgeree of seabass seared on a basket of kale.
(More truthfully scroungings from the wheelie at the Seagull Room.)
Now I'm planning my own series after the soaps.

But the current insists.
    Over the shoulder of the world it comes.
    And I who was sealed
    am a honeycomb.

A long way out.
        Oh never so far.
Over my head the butterfly is moving
away from the citadel and its arcades.
    Not that way, I want to shout,
that way is twenty miles without an orchid mouth.
But there it goes, as if it knew what I do not –
    black through my squint
and trembling
    like a sunspot.

Yes, I bartered my breath
for this. Here the sea's anaerobic
clerks tend their screens, every
molecule awarded its place,
never ending their trials at the terminals.

Now the sea drinks with me, bringing cup after cup.
What a night we have together, rolling in each other's arms.
And drowning's the second
impermissable dream. Each wave is a flume
and a fugue, high pressure August swell lifting me light
as the whipweed till each wave is a fog of dirty gold
where the swimmers are smiling with their cuttle teeth and then each wave
is a child at my ankle and then a mother to my mouth,

for her salt milk will make me strong as starfish,
as dead men's ropes, and I'm a belly bursting like a hot Dominican plum.
Here's the wine I wanted most and never was allowed.

At a Riverside Café in Užupis

for Michael Schmidt

We gather in the garden
where the river bucks and foams,
strangers come from the world over:
and this is our covenant –

> *tonight the cradle song*
> *tonight the bloody pastoral*
> *tonight the student with her bamboo flute*
> *tonight the wasp in the gall*

with all of us part
of the great accompaniment.

But asleep, awake,
it's much the same:
the sound of mother-of-pearl enters my ear
and I am a musician again
blessed by every note I left unstruck.

So I have rented a room
above the bar with a bed and a bleached desk
and not much more, and in the morning
there is black bread and raspberries
while outside the river
rises and the gypsy children
jump in their torn clothes from the bridge.
And yes, with the rest of them, I'm challenging the air.

It's in this part of the city
the anarchists sell their dark
smoke-tasting honey of oak flowers,
the labels hand-written on tiny pots.
And their paintings too stand by the bridge,
red and black studies in frames cut from pallets,
and woollen jerseys died with beetroot skins, and
children's toys of wood and twine,
puppets tied to the plane trees,
the anarchists' puppets painted
with crowns, ermine-necked, smiling.

Eventually I see this is where everyone arrives,
even the secret policemen who are out before dawn
searching for mushrooms in the forest
or gluing matchsticks to their model of the Manaus opera house.

Sometimes they stand here by the river
and hum the songs nobody wants to hear.
But these too have their places, and they sip their beers
according to the protocols.

While in church the
chanting the sweet
mist the man upon
the floor arms out
stretched I thought
angel in the gin
trap father I saw
him rise a golden
plover away even
though so rare
upon this moor

Tonight the symphony

> *tonight the knife thrower*
> *tonight the Arctic folksong*
> *tonight the orchestra*

and later I sit with the commissar
who grows garlic and every hour
barters one clove for one cup of coffee.
We hardly talk but watch the DJ who has set up in the garden
this May evening, the apple flowers
floating over our heads through his long trance track,
the lilac speeding like Stravinsky into the future,
the hundred-year-old lilac with the boom box in its cruck.
Because this is the place where people meet
to learn to sing again.
                    It's here we know
                    we're not alone.

The Minotaur

I see a rose
and I know this rose
is mighty. Not a petal
lifts when the Semtex goes
off. This rose
resists the partisan
and the patriot.
This rose
roars. This rose is its own
restoration. This rose
resumes. This rose
rules the savage garden.

Where Trafalgar's paths converge is a hollow tree.
In the dark the dealers stand around this sycamore
they have hacked, they have hieroglyphed, that is their totem.

At midnight they blink like turtles under their hoods.
Their language is a traffic of torchbeams and texts.
In the morning I step out to read their runes.

And this rose
resists uranium.
This rose repels
the clitorectomist's
spike. This rose sleeps
in the sandstorm.
This rose rejoices
in the aphid's tooth.
This rose is the refuge
and the refugee's
revenge. This rose
is the revolution.

I watch the schoolgirls kiss and their mouths are full of pebbles.
Each of them becomes a wave cupping its limestone dice.
When they take their driftwood home they will paint it gold.

A gale is blowing up in Trafalgar Wood
and I am a blind man rubbing my cheek against its hide

while sniffing the bloodstink of the wind.
Perhaps I have discovered the minotaur.

On the warden's digicam the orchids open Velcro mouths;
grass groans in its gridlock.
Then the Trafalgar branches spring to life
and I stand in a room full of clockwork.

Here the rose
returns. Its root revives.
This rose is the renegade
in the ranks. This rose
is the marvellous
maverick. This rose
resumes. This
is the rose after rot
and rout. This rose roars.
This rose is mighty.
This rose rules
the savage garden.

In a Fever Hospital

I come out of the wood
with my head on fire

And my mother places her nurse's hand upon my brow
and my father sits me down in the rocking chair

And asks, did you see the animals,
did you see the animals?

But all I know is the sunlight
is already turning to ashes in my head

And there is a steel reinforcing rod
pushing through the hollow of my spine

And I cannot speak
so they put me in a room behind a glass wall

Where I sleep and cry out
because there is the weasel

With his white magician's gloves
and there the viper

And out in the fields the cars are arriving,
the mothers delivering the children wrapped in linen,

Holding them to their breasts for the last time
like the long stems of roses,

The thorns clinging a moment
to their sleeves.

*

What's sleep
but a candle
lit under the sea?
This I dreamed in its light:

My heart has a history
    that is not mine.
My mind has a history
    that is not mine.
My bones have histories
    that they do not share with me.
Only my skin is faithful.
Flaying itself like a penitent
every
       seven
           years.

              *

There were fifty of us:
    fifty camellia flowers
lit on the bush before January was out,
fifty in our class, I say,
    and every face alive
after January's mildness and late tribulation.
Ha, the old mutilator could not find us.

    But February arrived
    with his measuring tape
    and the shears in his pouch.
Then March was whispering at the Stoneleigh Club,
    a schoolgirl in her first minidress
    and her face full of fish-hooks.

Now only I know what's to come.
I'm all that's left of fifty strong
and pledge here to tell our history,
for reason it might never be known.
Because April was waiting in his wheelchair,
that palsied boy with the big hands and ears.
    How he pulled at those wheelrims!
      Beware young April's snip snip,
      the clicking of his spokes.

Then there was May,
asleep in the shade under the hawthorn.
She was too small almost for the child-seat
in the silver Audi parked across the road

but was left there anyway
with the engine running.
One day I heard her crying
but nobody came,
the afternoon so hot
and the glass rolled tight to the rubber.
Sad little May who had woken too soon,
vowing her vengeance.

And June?
What was she
but the thrush egg,
the blue egg with the black star upon it
and the black sickle moon,
June as blue as the blue mosque at Babylon
where the dungbeetle preaches
to a congregation of stones.

July it finished.
But wasn't she there all the time –
a blood summer
when viruses linked arms
in swastikas?
I lost my mind in her maze
but remember the fall
and taking my place in the gallery.
Why did I fight so hard?
Here the sun cannot find me, nor the rain.
Maybe I'm becoming art:
Death's little masterpiece.

*

Drink, says the doctor of flesh and blood.
Drink, says the spirit doctor. Drink water.
We are made of water and must replenish our watery selves.

Now it falls from my forehead, tightens itself under my arms,
speaks volumes from my eyes and mouth.

So I drink water out of the tap, from plastic two–litre flagons,
from branded vials and vessels.

And here from the saucer of Ffynnon Pwll, a spring in the
dunes, where water rolls like a carriage through the ghost-train,
and by drinking, return myself to myself, restoring what has
been stolen from me.

Down here the water tastes of foxpiss and wild turnip,
of sheepdip and the lizard bones it carries away,
bones no stronger than the veins in a leaf,
of Ambre Solaire and tributyl chloride, of goat willow and
cuckoo spit, of Llew's takeaway pizza, the taste of the world like
a dirty knife against my teeth, a torrent out of the earth and out
of my hands
and against my chin.

Here comes water, it seems to say, subterranean and surrepti-
tious water claiming its birthright, spinning in that saucer,
tipping its brim and then racing out into the duneland, every
channel choreographed, every direction necessary, over to
where the archaeologists have cut their trenches, like the
soldiers before them, crouching in the valences as the targets
flashed by, down to where the lovers turned 360 degrees in the
dunegrass, for here comes water, imperious and common as
muck, water ecstatic at its own liberation – the remedial class
outside on the sunsoft tarmacadam – yes here it comes – the
football crowd through the café quarter, chairs upended, tables
smashed – water emerging out of the ground instead of us going
in, a runnel, a rivulet, a ruffian, a suffocation of water turning
everything the wrong way, then finding its balance, yes here is
water and I want to cheer the anarchy of water, that's what I
want to salute, its high tides, its low cunning, and here it is
again, cool to the fingertip, bluecold to the armpit, pouring out
of the saucer of Ffynnon Pwll, stored from the Ice Age in a
granary of water – that undiscoverable source – and every
second pumping through the ventricles in the limestone into
daylight, into twilight, and now over my shoes and out of my
hands, water the trailblazer, the map-maker, civilisation's lonely
scout, good health I say to its rites and riot, your very good
health, and the speedwell following its every move like a class-
room of blue eyes.

*

78

From the window I can see
this whole country:
    the House in the Speckled Land;
    Hammer Hill;
    the Rock of the Enchanter.

Next week, they promise,
I shall be released
to watch Europe
passing through an earthworm.

*

Delirium, darling, has its own rules.
When I said I loved you I was delirious.

When I said I needed you I was delirious.
When I spoke to you in Etruscan I was delirious.

When I said I am a murderer I was delirious.
When I said I lived in the Ghost Train I was delirious.

When I said I had counted the bricks of Babel
I was delirious. When I said I was delirious

I was delirious. When I said I was serious
I was delirious. When I said you were delectable

I was delirious. When I said your dithyrambs were a danger
I was delirious. When I said the dervishes

Deserved dessert I was delirious. When I said
I had a distemper this December I was delirious.

When I said the dye is deleterious to the dyer
I was delirious. But although I was delirious

I still dined at twilight with the disciples
And danced with the damselflies on Galilee.

Beware the delirious, my darling,
Who can distinguish the dreams from the dust.

*

Pop Quiz Tie Break. Who played the theramin
On *Good Vibrations*? Was it: a) Carl Wilson;
b) Dennis Wilson; c) Brian Wilson?

Answer? None of the above. Penalty: leave class
and follow me to the room behind the glass.
But don't ask how we get there, I don't know where to begin.

See here, from high on the pillows I can stare
at those who are afraid of my breath and my skin,
my ecosystem of contagious hair.

So look back with me at those I adore,
the king and queen, the mute with mandolin,
fixated with fever, that carnivore.

For this is my family, shy at the door
who have come to see crisis, my newborn twin
who lies with me now on the lonely moor,

And the minister too, and the mountaineer
and the meteorologist living in sin,
all touching the glass, and gazing, amazedly, in.

*

The dog is nearer now.

This grass is so tall I can see nothing beyond it, and even the
mound is invisible. Here gorse has laid its detonators across
what was the path and if anyone was left they would hear me
coming.

But I can't see anything and even the map shows only where the
mound used to lie because what I'm looking for is long
vanished.

The nearest ancient Britons now are the locals a mile away in
the pub, dark aborigines talking into their Nokias, legs crooked
as pitbulls', a Malibu bottle and its orange sun behind them
picked out in the dusk.

Slowly, you learn things. I was the man who rushed out of the house, soap on his ears, chasing after history. And what did I discover but the dog?

When the dog saw me it began to bark and advanced across the dune, a white dog becoming whiter, its jaws pink and stretched, a white dog with genes for gripping and not letting go, a fighting dog out of nowhere in the duneland that will soon be blue with buckthorn and move like water under the wind.

I looked at the dog and thought it something out of myself, larval, escaped from my cocoon, its mouth more alive than its eyes, a mouth like no other mouth I have seen, a mechanical mouth stronger than a bandsaw, and the rock I squeezed in my right hand was so hot surely I could see it glow through the bones of my fist.

The history I sought was an electrical notion. A vision, yes, a vision.
People lived here in Neolithic times, sucking the marrow out of deer bones. Looting their mound was never part of my plan. All I wanted was to lean against its side and press my ear to the sand and listen. And what would I hear but my own heart and the gorse unwrapping itself? Maybe the hum of the pipeline underneath the sand that takes the secret river away.

The people are gone, their language is gone, surely all that is left in that darkness are the roots of the grass. But over the dune the dog appears, a white guardian, shaking its voice between its jaws. Out of history the dog advances, emissary of the lost, its eyes red, its skin as pale as if it had emerged from three thousand years within the earth.

Now beside me the dog opens its mouth. I look in as if it is the entrance to the mound. Inside I can see the drinkers in their corners, the sand in the eyes of these regulars, and the landlord placing a bottle on the bar at the head of a line of bottles that vanishes into the dark...

*

I was the child who picked the lock of sleep.
And such a chamber I found –

Its rooftree the limb of a cedar of Lebanon,
and beyond that the sky

Where the hunter, the herdsman, the midnight swan
stared from their stations, stared down

At an altar where a light shone
the deadly white of the aconite

And in all that teetering hall
the fifty were lain upon its limestone

Pretending sleep, children with fingers
pointed under their chins with fringes thrown aside.

There they lay as figures, rapt, radiant,
drained the syrup from their spines,

A single drop of oil at a time,
an elixir necessary it was agreed

To translate fever's autobiography.
And I looked down upon myself and saw

The ant in his palace and all his sugar
furniture, the mirrors of carbon

Stretching along the corridors,
there being no end to the banqueting.

*

Teach me to walk.
Teach me to speak.
Pick me the iris leaf
that smells of the morgue
and grows on the moor.

Teach me to run.
Teach me to talk.
Catch me the cock linnet
with his bloody head
that lives on the moor.

Teach me the time.
Tell me the year.
Catch me the white badger
that lives on the moor
masked like the Lone Ranger.

Give me my words.
Give me my clothes.
Bring me the casket of rain
that shines on the moor.
That's where my reflection goes.

*

Round here there's never enough darkness left:
the malarial weekend fizzes out of a can;
there's a worm in the bottle of Saturday night.

One thousand in the cinema queue
for *Lord of the Rings*, as the One Ring's
ultra-violet beam tilts over the Odeon.
There were fifty of us once in the vanished wards
and such a power of dreaming we had –

fifty faces pale with the effort
of conjuring the creatures out of ourselves.

Now what's that sound? The curlew, the ambulance,
or our own ghost voices in the corridors

returning through the night's cortex, fifty shocked
beings in their smocks

at the windows like fifty stems of grass
lying down together as the wind blows through.

Photographing an Orchid

I knelt in the chalk
to talk to the orchid

and what was she
but an Albanian girl
in her headscarf
in the quiet corner of the playground.

Or so I thought.

And I searched for the notes –
the possibles, the impossibles
that might go between us.

Yet this year
    as every year;
this summer as ten thousand summers
    the chalkland courtesan
dismisses her own resurrection
amongst the ghost corals and all the failed fossil regimes
as if the scripture of science might explain her life away.

In her memory hoard
is ice's tabernacle that covered this plain,
the crocodilian shore.
But no boast.
    Or botany.
Only being.
    Her venom, deadly to me,
    is indifference.

    So here she is,
the bee orchid on her prehistoric plinth,
a bee orchid black and gold, a lacquered music-box.
But when I enter her and touch the springs and see
the fangs retract and the pollen pulleys release their grip
and her shaft reveal itself through elevator doors,
when the secret drawer in the secret drawer opens
    what's there but a mirror
    that shows only
    my own surprise.

Eventually I had come
to a field full of flowers.
Each one had its head bitten off.
How still they were, a crowd
frozen into a moment of
forgetting, while around us
the electric fence
was all the horizon we'd need.

Now, my mother is hissing
in her kitchen, the taps
drumming in the sink to hide
her own torrent of words.
Again, again, that spectral
whisper – the sounds through
the water naked now but
unashamed, her throat a clock
wound too tight, her words the willow
whitening in the slack, aimed at the world
by the demon in her
whose face is not hers
and whose voice is not
hers, but whose rage I have felt
pricked on the roll of that music-box
and whose skin is harder and whiter
than the sea holly I must
hold no matter
it leaves me raw.

    There are things
we cannot learn, having
no way of breaking their code.
But listen long enough you'll hear
a hawk hatched from a lark's egg.

    Kneeling, focusing,
I watched the pill
undissolve itself on her tongue,
all the Bronze Age parade itself backwards
on the Buccaneer's big screens.

    Clever, she is;
I'll give her that:

what it has cost me to come to her, over
barbed-wire and buckthorn, pushing through
the darknesses in a city of hemlock,
a refugee myself, whose skin crawls, whose shirt
is shredded on his back, and the ants
airborne already, hot from their foundry,
swimming through my hair.

There was all manner of machination
around me as I stepped into the light,
a buzzard afloat
in his blue senate,
and the queen bee
surrounded by drones,
somnolent, huge
as a silver
airbag.

So I lie with the Olympus
and the isotronic cola
in its gourd. And testify:

In the womb
of her mind
grew the demon.

I fed him.
I sang to him.
Soon his head

was too heavy,
his wings iron
and velvet,

his bones
the sunless side
of June grasses.

Stillborn
I thought him.
But his way was lit.

Now here I lie,
my heart to her earth and my left eye
closed. Yet it's my life that's shown
within the black shutter
which is no door into her subterranean seminary,
and neither the nautilus nor the lover nor the laptop lepidopderist
can remember the password to her intranet.
This lens I carry
will send the bee orchid round the world in forty seconds,
but whether perfect
or imperfect
who could ever tell?

To Those on the Promontory

The sky is arriving:
> blood in the egg:
snow on the ghost train roof.

Do you know what I like about this town?
> Fat Tuesday.
Even when the fair is closed
and these days the fair is usually closed
> it's Fat Tuesday.
Yes that's what I like about this town.

And this morning the sea paved
lilac. After the harrowing night.
> Not an inch of swell
> not a fleck
but the cuttle ashore already in stooks,
> cuttle for sale
> cuttle cuttle
from the cuttlemonger's castle.
> The skeletons of the surf.

Wake now.
> Please wake.
It is 4 a.m. and the letters are waiting in their honeycomb.
Mothman's mother places the milk
at his bedside. Such a calligrapher he is, those labels
in cabinets ablaze with his captures.
She thinks of him in the summer dusk
hanging his lamp under the oak.
How quickly the glories come to him,
the folds of his uniform crackling with wings,
the censer swinging, flakes
of the evening falling out of the sky,
but pretty pinion, northern drab,
who else could know their genealogy
but her gentle son?
Above his head
the seraphim
fly forever
across the formaldehyde moon.

Who was out last evening
                but the Worm
with his lurcher, his small change rosary,
his British sherry secret-throated
          under the pharmacy architrave?

Who else would we find in this doorway
          with the town bent double
          under the hurricane
      and Sker's pillars
      become headless statues,
          bulletholed, leadshot scattergunned,
its warriors molluscs,
its music a supper chant
as the rockpools' bedlamites banged spoons on bowls,
who else but the Worm
in the pride of his penitence?
      Twice a day there's revolution here.

          Dear Ceridwen Williams,
did you feel *Estoril* rock on its bricks last night
as if the wind pulled it across the point,
its undercarriage a tutu of sparks,
your sheaves of sheet music shooting a hundred feet into the air?

Now at 7 a.m.
beyond your caravan
the sea is a glazed
Babylonian tile.

A caravan, Ceridwen?
Your parents' eyes would narrow in contempt.
But you slept in a country ages away
and awoke to a Teasmade of Earl Grey.
So how many recorder concertos are there in your repertoire?
This morning you play the 'Goldfinch'
which can never
can never be right
but you smile to yourself at such twittering.
As if last night brought more to the minister's daughter
than a glass of white wine mixed with soda water.

But often there comes a someone else.
Sometimes that someone is mild and sometimes mad,
chewing samphire fingers for the citric aftershock,
convinced of the telepathy of stones.
And sometimes he's the beachcomber
who sits on Sker with his ear to the rock
listening to saltwater pour through the passageways below.
Sker, he's learned, is the limestone egg
that fills with the sea's white embryo.

He's the servant of Sker, he's scalded by it,
its sketcher, its sculptor
this scout, this scion, this cuttlemongrel
and counterfeiter of the driftwood gospel,
scat singing to the tide's scansion,
seaweed widower, the scarred,
the scarifier, the master of all salt ceremonies
and scrutiniser of its schools of sacrifice,
this savant who scoffs at me daily, scolding me
for sitting in the window while the sea
is scheming to scroll its scars upon my skin
and the stars to start their skirmishing in the dark bayous.

Jizz does wraps
does lids
doesn't do scag
at the corner by the Kingdom of Evil
and sometimes he hears voices when he's walking home
a curlew
          calling
                    curfew
canticle for lost souls
the curlew music he always knew was there
as something in himself
while the current in Gwter Fawr paces back and forth
like the father he is afraid to become.

British Airways vapour tree:
the sky in X-ray:
snow on the ghost train roof.

          Look here.
It's Mrs Dawes-Llewellyn,

to the manner born
and more roughly rouged than a cock pheasant.
   Her grandfather was a sea captain
and she wears the necklace of pumice stone he brought from St Helena.
      Ah, Dorothy Dawes, Dorothy Dawes,
         the collar of black pearls upon your neck,
with your Nivea, your Nurofen,
your hair the year-round hebe with its blue sea-fret,
      who but you
knows the colour of Porthcawl is the wave's
portcullis that splinters on the breakwater,
      imprisons the heart,
who but you this morning
saw the nun on fire lead her greyhounds through the town?

My advice?
Love the lavender.
Leave it lie.
Out of the rift it comes.
Nothing grows closer to the wave.
Even the tide cannot suck its secret out.

So now do you know what I like about this town?
      Fat Tuesday.
Even when the fair is closed
and these days the fair is usually closed
      it's Fat Tuesday.
And that's what I like about this town
where the road ends, where the road is ending
and we are on the promontory.

The Worm has the weather forecast
written in his eyewhites.
It's Lundy force nine forever
but there is lightning too, lightning like
lug–silver hauled hissing out of the ground.
The ocean's transformer stands behind its razorwire
and everyone in town last night electrical-convulsive,
strapped to their beds.
      But this morning
      not an inch of swell
      not a fleck.

All hail helios
say the doomwatchers to the dogwalkers
and the horizon aches like a paper cut.

Down Rhych Avenue I think it was
I shone my torch around a cave:
            isopods scittered,
there was a tear duct in every gryke.
              And that's where I saw them,
the paintings the current had left;
    stick men and stags,
    and our sun with its green helix
    in a core sample of fossilised light.
The sea's scrimshaw maybe,
as if we lived our lives upon a narwhal tusk,
this town where the road ends, is ending now,
where we are on the promontory.

    Last night under the breakwater
while the dark double bassists were sawing with their limestone arms
and the conductor brandishing his pincers at the air
      each wave was a white
      was a white
      carnation the orchestra
      had trodden underfoot
as Grace Williams with her book of children's psalms
      drowned in a lobster-pot.

Because the sea's the only maestro here.
John the Song auditioned for *Pop Idol*
but his voice trembled like meadowsweet
in the Salt Lake car park. And anyway
    as he would say
    this is all
    this is all of it
    light opera.

Now there's NV,
             old NV with his metal detector.
    Another sweep this morning
but the fabulous hoard does not stir the dial.
NV has read of chariots unearthed
with the skeletons of gold-corseted kings

still holding the rawhide reins.
   He brings his grandson
   but the boy is soon bored.
I think we're looking in the wrong place, Aled.
Not a doubloon, not Lord Caractacus's iron crown,
not a ringpull. Only the lugubrious
   lug at their libations
   knotted in the bait bucket,
foaming with a language that needs no oxygen.

But we have this in common:
we have run out of country.
We have this in common:
we have come to the chasm-mouth.
And that is what I like about this town.

Listen to what John sang. How the judges squirmed:

Walk through the door of mother-of-pearl,
walk through the ashen wood.
The sea will keep us under its wing
for we were born its brood.

Try putting a drum machine under that, John told them.
But steel plate? Our tropic garden. Luscious
as lichen the orange oxides grow.
How the town bleeds under its winters.
It's a wounded gangster disguised as an insurance salesman.

8 a.m.
Read the small ads lately?
Mothman seeks the tawny wave,
the bordered gothic.
          Mothman WLTM
a scarlet tiger or small chocolate tip.
Mothman desires the clouded magpie, the poplar kitten.
And Mothman will die happy to record
as twilight oozes from the dunes
the confused
or the suspected
taking to the wing.
          Oh Lord, as the tide comes in
          and light is lost
          is that too much to ask?

He has seen them in smocks and
cassocks, on catwalks and catafalques,
in kilts and kaftans and jalabiyas
with hearts upon their sleeves and kohl upon their eyes,
singing in the chorus at the Grand Pavilion
and reading the news on CNN.
Once he carried a candle through Candleston
and a kitchen maid kissed his hair.
He has curtsied upon a quilt of canaries
and crawled before an emperor.
As he said last week in 'The Lorelei' –
who does not love lepidoptera does not love life.
 And one day the pale
 prominent in her
 wedding-veil
 will be waiting
 in Trafalgar Wood.

Now Dorothy Dawes, Dorothy Dawes,
your pampas grass is a barrel of saws.
There's a marine morning climbing in your blood
white as the panicles of the Russian vine.

Here you stand with your silver trowel
looking east, looking west,
the volcano seeds upon your breast.
There's mother-of-thousands in the clints
and spurs on the waves where the steelworks glints.
 If no one was looking
  where would you dig?
Quickly, Dorothy, put flower and root
on life support in your Shogun boot.
They grant you this alternative
to the fossil's frosted clockwork in the cliff.

  Jizz knows the tide
will come further in than this
and not even Tricky, not even all
the remix masters there have ever been
can lay him low like that curlew calling
    nearly
   nearly
  nearly
   nearly
    nearly.

He sits in the empty Embassy
watching *Apocalypse Now*,
its fire-eggs in their hatcheries,
his lips as yet too thin to kiss
his newborn son, a red
chilli in its cellophane.
The road ends, is ending here
and he is on the promontory,

You're thinking again, NV,
of the tasselled caps in the glass cabinet at school.
Don't you know thinking is bad for us?
But with *Ich Dien* spelt upon your heart
you guessed you were the man apart.
Better to look at the cormorant, NV,
        there is one only,
a black singularity
        abob in the wave's scrape.
Herald of loneliness that Sker crow
might still teach you the meaning of escape.
Or maybe you think you've got it made
pacing round your penthouse on the Esplanade.

Between *Estoril* and the point
sand's an esker and escalator :
and there's music:
the boy delivering the *Daily Mail* stops to listen:

it's that weird Miss Williams with some kind of flute
waltzing around in her birthday suit

whilst Vivaldi sits on a thistle head
whistling until his cheeks turn red.

All hail helios
Hail his golden haul
cries Ceridwen.

Everywhere are her earthquakes –
the rotted teeth
                the collapsing breasts
but only such landslides can reveal
                the lode.

This morning nothing will separate her
from the season's C major caress
as sunlight licks the libretto on her cuttlebone.

All you people
all you people waiting here
you are writing your names
you are writing your names
in the snow on the ghost train roof.

We have this in common:
we all have this:
the road ends, is ending here
and we are on the promontory.
We all have this in common:
we all have this:
we have come to the chasm mouth.
Even in broad daylight you will feel the night sweats here.
The heart like limestone itself falls sheer away.

Return of the Natives

M4 Jct 36
could be I'm home

could be this is it with all
the purple moor grass

swathed like Odeon u/v over
the fast food factories

because on the hard
shoulder KFC nugget

bucket so could be I'm
here could be Screen 6

next week showing sunset
over bluebell reef bleached

white yeah could be I'm
back could be supplementary information

exists could be I never
left but fell asleep to awake as

married segment control information exists
in retail park hard shoulder wedding

could be I never left my beautiful
life could be I dreamed

almost everything
because I tell you what my trouble is my

trouble is I forget nothing that's always been my
trouble and what kind

of life is that for a
man so just smash it all up into tiny dark splinters please

2

Swallows on the rafter;
a barn door never closed
and a shape that could have been a man.

But light's the revolution here
with dust so thick in the beam
I might think people
were building themselves out of the sunsmoke:

men and women with eagle faces,
all the griffin-lords of Babylon
stepping down from temple walls,
or a commuter crowd on the escalator
whose covenants are packed
into a valise, a rucksack sewn
with the wreath of the zodiac.

But now I know I am that dust
and here I go, streaming away from myself
in a torrent that might pass through steel or stone,
and I am not the swallow
    but its flight
and not the hand or what it held
but the air that hand hastened
into a fire of photons.

And at last there he is,
    the minotaur
     cracked on his rope,
all the centuries of grass
burning under his feet.

3

One day a woman knocked at my door.
She said she had once lived in this house

and showed me the traveller's altar
she carried, no bigger than a hotel matchbook,

the haloes around Christ's hands
as if he was holding fireworks.

But in my study she walked a crazy-paving of books
that led her astray from herself;

in my bedroom she could not even recognise
the shape of the air

or the ghost of whom she might have been –
a girl with her eyes squeezed shut in prayer –

God bless Mammy, God Bless Dada.
But now there is no one left to bless

and in the kitchen there was nothing to remember.
But I tried to see with that girl's eyes

and there on the board were the halves of a lemon
scraped white of their zest:

two cups that lay like a girl child's breasts,
the knife between.

A Porthcawl Dolphin

The sea in an hour falls forty feet.
When it is safe I come out of my cupboard in the cliff,
this cave the hyenas want to take from me.
One day their bones will lie soft as thistledown here
under these animals on the cave walls,
alive in the ochre I mix, the creatures yet to come.

So I step out to find what I know is there.
Up on the ledges under the crest, under
the lavender that lies in petrol pools,
the ocean is falling through these crevasses
like some service elevator filled with laundry bags.
And no, it will not take long.

There it is, the sea-calf,
hooves still bound in their white bootees.
But to me it is a little skewbald foal
the dam had dropped in this desert and left a week ago.

Already the bone of its beak is yellow as bamboo,
already my familiar is a temple
for the bottlegreen crabs of this place, forgotten,
almost unreachable this place, the crabs with their eyes
on lightning rods, crabs come with ratchets and claws
like pearl-handled derringers, come with their cold blood's appetite that
can never be sated in these limestone malls
blue under the moon, these crabs, jewelled and furtive.

For the future belongs to them.
I have painted them in my homestead,
these sea-sawyers stealing from every salt-stoppered
limestone stoup, from rock pools like immersion tubes,
from black bayous where the sun's systole has ceased.
And look: how they grip their ground.

My shadow is nothing to them now.
How they swivel when they feel my step, their sensors in a switchboard,
their eyes a morgue
of diamonds under the thrift.
Yes, I could sweep them from this ledge
no wider than the shelf where my books wait.
But tomorrow they will be redeemed and ready with their remedy.

The Fairground Scholar

your name upon my belly
your e-mail on my breast
when you carve your X upon my tongue
I'll know that I can rest

Now

can't feel your
                    pulse
can't taste your
                    dialect
can't follow your
                    gospel
can't read your
                    palm
can't remember
                    what I
can't remember
                    what it was I
wanted to say
                    but surely
it's what the
                    god of yellow
said to the
                    god of blue
there must be
                    green gods
too my sister
                    there must be
green gods too

Okay
we are doing it
your way: watching
the storm destroy its text,
the tattooist become his own prosody,
ants conspire on the forest floor
in syllables of carbon and hydrogen,
the child emerge from the surf
with all the tide's codes broken in her head;

Orion haul the empty cars around the SkyMaster;
the indicative being taken into custody,
Class A words bought and sold in the Buccaneer,
a baby born at the side of the road
and anointed with the black language;
video games reciting the Iliad,
the Dalai Lama gathering up the jackpot in the Hi-Tide arcade,
Rimbaud's black and green vowels marching out of Somalia to meet him,
the drowning man arguing semantics with the sea.

But don't you know how dangerous
        this type of thing can be?

I found you in the fairground
waiting for the ghost train to open its doors:
you were working out the bibliography of sand
but I took the dictionary from your lap
and all the reference pages from your hand
and rolled you up
        and packed you away
until the start of the new season
when the siren sounds
    and ghosts walk in the labyrinth
and you have forgotten all about
running off with the the circus folk.

So dream a little. The caff's art deco;
and outside it's Trieste not Trecco.
The arm of the Atlantic round your waist.

Though you seem to be a terrible flirt
there's no reason why you should get hurt:
the arm of the Atlantic round your waist.

Here's George W. Bush, come up from the ranch.
He'd like to beat us to death with an olive branch.
The arm of the Atlantic round his waist.

While under the urn staring out at the rain
Is our Kingdom of Evil's Saddam Hussein.
The arm of the Atlantic round his waist.

You see. I've invited all these friends –
just so we can make amends.
The arm of the Atlantic round your waist.

But maybe it's better to keep your eyes closed
like every good girl knows she's supposed;
the arm of the Atlantic round your waist.

Then you and I in this corner seat
will never have a problem with the ghosts we meet.
The arm of the Atlantic round your waist.

Over at the counter is Richard Burton,
a vector of vodka, a final curtain.
The arm of the Atlantic round his waist.

You know the type – such radiant addiction –
victims who can't tell fact from fiction.
This arm of the Atlantic round his waist.

That's just what I like about the fair –
all the famous faces you can spot round here:
the arm of the Atlantic round your waist.

     But listen.
      I come from the carnival.
I know its people and what they'd do
if they saw what's in your mind.

Now in my desk you lie awake –
your mind a Californian motel room
with the tv on
              the shower on
                        the refrigerator door
open

        and you cross the parking lot
            in the sweet evangelical rain
        that's bringing up all the golden irises
          across the desert floor
and you rent that room for one more night
and from there you post your library
one book at a time

across the continents:
the pages you scattered on the bed
                    lifting in the breeze
like feathers on the breasts of Mojave doves.

You say
a day is coming
when I won't prevent
you becoming your own text.

Confront, you will say,
the sea's error:
how to read it;
how to learn from it;
how to avoid being swept away,
the sea's eternal error
that has kept so many this peninsula's prisoner.

Then tomorrow you will sit in the Anchor bar
with a rummer of soda and lime

and afterwards, make an expedition
to the paper beach, the beach of rust,

the beach where the sand has thinned
so all the ribs of the wreck are exposed:

the wreck that looks like thirteen black bowmen,
black arms raised, firing into the sun.

And maybe in a little while you'll return to these arcades –
a manuscript now so full of words –

and the readers will come and speculate
on how a manuscript writes itself:

the words that haunt, the words that teach,
the words that must overreach;

all the unspeakable acts of words
that we keep behind the glass.

So what is it I'd learn from you?
That in this place two paths exist:

or a forking path of fevers
one of which we choose.

Maybe. But think harder and you'll see
the nails unhammer themselves

from the floorboards, and the yellow
unpaint itself from the wall

while in the garden behind the fair
the little appletree turns itself

inside out. And suddenly is as pale as my mother
stepping from her bath.

That foam on her face
and on her breasts

is the appleflowers
flying into the air.

They are all our mothers,
those little appletrees,

their appleflowers whitening
an orchard of wet skin.

But hush...
come further... come still further in...

there's so much more of your fortune that I can tell.
See... here are the horses... the horses on the carousel...

horses... dream horses...
Mary and Madeleine and Nathaniel...
horses... dream horses...

round and round in the head...
horses... dream horses...
Mary and Madeleine and Nathaniel...

teeth bared... eyes polished
by the girl with the hump under her hair...
the girl who rides the carousel

and calls the horses… calls to the dream horses…
Mary and Madeleine and Nathaniel…

Stop.
Here's a corpse.
Look at the label on its big toe:
Global Foundry Company, Cardiff.
Property of the British Empire.

So smell the crowd
at this autopsy, craning in its ranks
as the surgeon cuts
the Y into the thorax

and the page of the face
is peeled back and there's
the heart suddenly
black as an aubergine.

Listen to the gasps.
Such fools. As if the saw
of schizophrenia had not
already done this work
or gin provided
a glossary on the tongue's
sole.

       Believe me.
I stood in attendance
as the surgeon carved a butterfly
out of the air.

But have they anywhere stated
the cause of death?

Old age?
Drowning?

Spanish flu?
Barbiturates? Exhaustion?

Thirst? Disbelief? Happiness?
Hepatitis? Avalanche? Dementia?

Demoniacal possession? Carbon monoxide? Sunburn?
Lung cancer? Heavy metal? Religion? Self abuse?

Patricide? The state's neglect? High tar? A meteorite?
White bread? Civil war? Hodgkin's Lymphoma? Tesco's Vladivar Vodka?

Anaphylaxis?
Shyness?

Such is the chorus
from death's thesaurus.

Though the result's the same
you must give it a name.

And that barking?
It's the fairground dogs as the moon comes up
between the Megablitz and the SkyMaster.
It's moon matrimony.

And all the world's dogs
bred from three Chinese wolves –
three Neolithic bitches seduced
by the moon rising in each other's eyes.

Your name upon my belly
your e-mail on my breast
when you carve your X upon my tongue
I'll know that I can rest.

Here we can watch the dwarf
give birth to the giant

and the mermaid marry the cannibal.
Beware, there are all kinds of people here:

look at the man who had a camera placed
in his coffin. In death, a sensation,

as never in life. See on the screen
the extent of his corruption:

how his face falls away from itself
like the Somerset coast: how

his toenails become
ribs of iridium.

There he lies,
busied in his mansion. But the people walk past

to the artist, swinging in his harness
as he paints the *Welcome* sign

and under the tarpaulin someone is hanging
across the Grand Canyon.

But close your eyes,
here's my surprise.
The arm of the Atlantic round your waist.

Corner seat, Blue Dolphin café –
have you guessed the reason we're here today.
The arm of the Atlantic round your waist.

There's Agamemnon in his golden mask:
no use offering him our thermos flask.
The arm of the Atlantic round your waist.

At the first table are the Three Graces
with henparty hungover faces.
The arm of the Atlantic round your waist.

But listen to the Stones sing 'Satisfaction':
trust an old juke box to give us some action.
The arm of the Atlantic round your waist.

That *I can't get no* always gets me,
but it's even better if somebody lets me.
The arm of the Atlantic round your waist.

So here's my number marked in foam.
Is it a problem if I walk you home,
the arm of the Atlantic round your waist?

If we run away it'll seem slow motion,
but why buy a drink when you can swallow an ocean?
And that's the tongue of the Atlantic you can taste.

Sageflowers for Charles Saatchi

Yes it's late
but will Mr Saatchi take the call?

It is the moment before nightfall:
slick on her mousepad and somnolent in dew
the slug waits for dark's antibodies
to grow into her grooves.
See how she moves, snubbing the sun.
Soon the night, that lover, that acrobat
will jump through her lariat.

But something is happening
behind our backs.
The evening becomes the sky
and the sky becomes the church
and the sandstone stoup by the church door
becomes the rain barrel
and when June
dissolves itself in the barrel
its water turns the colour of sageflowers.

Can you see them, Mr Saatchi?
Are you taking this in?
The sageflowers are the June evening
pulled inside out, as the yellowhammer's thread
of magma shoots whitehot from the dune.

But focus on the rain barrel, the barrel where a woman
reaches down. She is the last one here tonight
and almost invisible at her water work,
her jets rolling over the sand like tiny ballbearings.
It is she who has let the sageflowers surge against the sun
as if she were some Zuni
mistress of turquoise;
or, if she has given them thought at all,
left them to riot in their wisdom and their woad.

I would give you such sageflowers, Mr Saatchi,
all the indignant
indigos of their apotheosis,

so that you might place them
against a white metropolitan wall
in a sepulchre of bulletproof perspex
with a Securitas ex-Para in a FCUK tie
to stand them guard
and we could honour the sageflowers, Mr Saatchi,
and the sageflowers would teach us how to pray
   together in their temple.

Because on the screen of your Samsung
you can watch the woman who grew them,
the woman whom I am recording for you, Charles,
that woman in the shadow of St John's,
the water an arm's length down, blood
warm to her elbow but cooling
as she sinks her skin into the barrel,
colder now because always in that barrel
the Brythonic embryos of ice survive the sun,
and the further she reaches the colder it becomes,
because by now her feet have almost left the ground
and her face is touching the surface,
half her body within the barrel
as if she was reaching into the earth itself.

   I know, Charles,
     the sageflowers are almost black
but a June evening is never completely dark.
Now the woman is reaching as far as she can reach,
as if she would pull the drowned head of the December god
out by its hair, the god with his clenched and newborn face,
his hair the feathers of the swift that fell into the barrel,
the swift dead in its immortal hour,
the god's eyes sealed, the god's voice shackled,
the god's lips the wings of the moth that fell into the barrel,
the moth a little gold archbishop
drowned in its vestments,
and the woman reaching into the barrel
as if she would hold the god's head up as a trophy
and shake it, Charles, shake it as a dog might shake itself,
to make the god roar,
yes make him
roar.

Paradise

Above me the sparrow
and above the sparrow

the shape of the hawk,
the sparrowhawk itself.

But how soon the sky is emptied of both
the sparrow and its terrorised song.

Yet one drop of blood
has fallen onto my hand

and I carry it gravely like a child
wanting a father's word for some unworded thing,

evidence, surely evidence,
though of what he will now never say,

and soon I am on the summit of the dune
and out on the ocean

I see the altars of rain
from which shapes of birds are rebounding

as if from a forcefield, black
sparks from the black

conflagration of rain coming my way
at such a speed the eye can hardly take it in

and now that black rain
is falling and the black shapes of birds,

sparrows and sparrowhawks, crying in their outrage,
and there's lightning like the circuitry, botched,

modern, fed through a medieval mosque,
and how soon it is twisting around me, the storm's black

jalabiya, and the rain looking like
some ziggurat the dictator

demanded built, a black and empty
tower where the rain twists itself

in handfuls of black roots
ripped from this earth,

and the storm's a perfect cylinder
contructed by the mechanics of the air

and I think surely if there are paradigms
of paradise they are found

within the storm's anterooms,
lit now only

by the black light of its rose-window,
for now it's a cathedral that's passing overhead,

a supersonic corral
of prayer with the sound of choirs shouting their amazement

and the rain crackling like soldered rods
as if the stones on this summit

were still hot from their first configuration,
and then it is gone, growling into the north, gone from the dunes,

the storm headed north,
and who were they, I wonder,

the man in the black coat with the child
in her black hood under his arm

who brushed past when I could not move
or even stand for rain

leaving me behind and my sky
and my skin and my voice gnawed white.

The Weighbridge

Praise the tooth that bites the tongue.

So out I go into the thickening,
the storm light fraught, a fret upon the town.

Two hours later here's me licked.
Sky is a greatcoat over the day
and I'm drenched in the drumlins
with willows' verdigris.

But something is watching.
Something knows I am here.
It sees me move through this mere,
black rain in my face, me a swollen creature,
eyes ashiver, hair in thorns, forlorn but unfallen, yes that's me,
but a snip, a snap in that snipe's eye.
Too near, too near.

        So up goes the marsh goat
with all its names in pursuit, bird of a hundred names
and those names following like buckshot
but never getting close,
white stripe of a snipe from the wet,
that snipe in a strop, dusk on us already,
the blackthorn unbecoming itself, the moon
lost but a last light on the pools like Tudor's
tin-topped desk, his dockets on a spike,
and outside in the hutch the kid who worked
the weighbridge, hundredweights in his hands
for the gangers under the gantry where the shears hung.

And on this day that is no day
I wave to myself, that child I was, perfectly absorbed,
pencilling the figures for the precious-metal shop,
for I was that tyro who toted tons, the iron
in its fealty coming my way, the gypsy
iron both honest and plundered,
being exactly what I said it had to be.

To the ounce, Mr Fury. The veritable ounce.
That was our oath. To the last sprockle of rust
I paid them what was owed
for Mary Ann Street guttering and a Humber's blistered chrome.

Pisspoor those scrapmen looked,
but from the wads waved at the braziers
ruination was not so raw.

Thirty years ago that was;
swarf a frost where snipe snickered on the morfa,
the evening blue as oxyacetylene,
me shutting the books,
last cargo of the day a transit limping in.

The Saint of Tusker Rock

I served the surf.
I suffered it.

A saviour, I thought,
a form in the foam,

some message that was
mine and meant for me.

What arrived was a ship
whose men spoke like gulls,

not bothered about gods, only the eel
they saw in my smokery,

a conger black and
gold and grinning on its
gallows. Strong meat,

but in their firelight we were
souls together sharing

a cup, safe for a night
and sure, at least, of that.

So many strangers but I remember them all.
Broken by thirst they would stagger ashore
to my freshwater spring. When they had drunk
and fallen asleep I could look into their faces
        and see their dreams.
So why was it then I never thought my own well could run dry?

2

Apprentice to salt,
I come from a vanished church.
While I swim my sackcloth swings on seakale;
a leathery man, you'd say, his mouth the imperial
purple of the whinberry.

Yes
they tell stories about:
a castaway naked on the rock
waving the driftwood between his legs –
that old goat's greeting to his god.

A child lives with me.
No novice, she has ten summers and eleven winters
and was picking damsons in the dunes
when she saw the wolves in single file come through Cwm y Gaer,
the pack nose to tail,
one's paws perfect in the pawprints of the next,
their pelts of limestone, of seawater.
For a while she stayed with me, blithe and bonny,
my little belter who speaks the old language,
her breasts hard as fennel bulbs,
whispering like sand into my ear
her words for darkness, her barbarous words for prayer.

3

Everything you have I foresaw:
My mirror is the mother-of-pearl's mist upon the palm.

That's how I watched Stonehenge go by
on its rafts, the bluestones coming
out of the west, lashed with hemp.
And maybe they waved –
those oyster-eaters, those temple sailors –
and began to dream of Babylon.

Later, I sat in the Plaza for the first night
of *Silence of the Lambs*.
Anthony Hopkins was our local boy

made good, but half way through
I noticed his eyes were
dead. And I realised
that where there is no god
man must pray to a stone.

4

Now outside in Llewellyn Street
sulphur slurs the air
and slovens sleep through Sundays.
Whether we wake or not
Silurians ever ever ever
shall be slaves.

So who will be our Spartacus?
                    It is getting late.
But I smile when I think of Kirk Douglas
with the star-shaped dimple in his chin
like a bullet hole or a cleaned out cancer cut.
I heard him roar in the Plaza's thrilling dark
but cannot remember now if he was crucified or not.

5

        In the bay
I swam beside a basking shark
        and in its eye
glimpsed the first day of this world.
        It too is praise
        of paradise.

But should I ever trust the sea?
Every day a different bride:
the oyster-thief, the samphire
turning red,
        the surfer who is
a ghost on the slipway,
exquisite through mist
his contemplation of these waters.
But that whisper of delirium,

right, left, above my head?
Ah, the goldfinches
in the grykes, in the black
arms of the bittersweet,
in limestone's menagerie
of extinctions. Yes, the goldfinches
of the clifftop, gone like courtesans
gossiping to bed.

Now at dawn I look from
my attic. Well here's a cold
crucifixion. The night's tide
has brought the jellyfish in.
There lies one, snake
in a wine glass, the foetus
of a stone. But something molten
lingering at its crater, and in the void
where the heart should be, and about its
outflung arms. Such
an experiment of being
that the sea delivers to my feet.
And who but I to greet our visitor,
this thalidomide child upon
the sand, a broken carafe
the wave sweeps away

6

After years of gardening here's what I recall:
to thrive the soul needs a soul-facing wall.

I made this home
where the earth ends
 – a bivouac beside St John's –
and watched it fill with red beanflowers that the bees love,
red as the bees themselves.

The rain barrels were brimful in the Baptist's garden
which once was my chosen church.
I can stand by the beans I planted and see
in this pod's white pith a pulpit
where a furious fruit is announced.

Then Monday night bell practice starts simple
but soon the changes challenge my own rhythms
as the bells are opening and closing
like the Baptist's marigolds in the dusk,
time racing until it's dawn-dusk in seconds,
daylight for a moment and then the dark again
and the bells' vines vanishing under my skin
and the bells' perfume soaking my skin
like the iron-coloured gooseberries waiting in wine.

7

On the highest ridge
I pricked my girl child's skin
with the tattoo of a blue hare.
    And ordained:
she shall be swift:
she shall lie open-eyed under the moon:
she shall not linger long in her whirlpool of grass.

These days I walk the coast alone
and feel my mind skip like a stone –

the grey, the green, the amethyst
of the rock pool's eucharist.

Yip, there's a thousand tracks on that iPod
and every one the word of God.

So too is there life in a lightless wood.
Look at the honeysuckle's circuitry:
it spirals out of the earth and shows where the power will travel
        and how it will move.
Soon there's a canopy where the leaves will press
in passover and a buzzard at roost on that reef of leaves
    never knowing I stand below
        and see into the hurricane of its eye.

8

But mine is the vanished church.
My cathedral? A quiver of sticks.
    I took it down,
    laid it low
    in the sandy tilth,
the roof beam, the spandrels, the flying buttresses
where at the last hung only ivy of sea-mist.

While the garden filled with fruits
the beansticks were a belfry of bees.
But that pyramid now is a pyre beside St John's,
and the bells' music a lorrypark throb
or a rain of horseshoes or oranges or broken black umbrellas,
each bell an engine of ecstasy its bellman would say,
though I think the bells are chess played in the sky,
or mathematics, which always had a mosquito sound for me,
but now is bellmetal in this bellyard.

9

I watched my child place a seed in the ground.
Only we knew the place and only we knew the secret.

We watered it.
Something started to grow.
Who would believe a stone when a leaf astonishes?

First day:
dew's duty done:
Rust already on the rose.

Second day:
the infinitesimals
building.

Third day:
look aside once and your software is out of date.
Nothing stops now.

Fourth day:
breathe the avalanche: grass is speeded up:
This is what a miracle means.

Fifth day:
locusts. We're refugees
upon the highways of the leaf.

Sixth day:
harvest. While the world's computers
write a new gospel.

Seventh day.
In darkness we bury ourselves without blessing –
who waited too long for our lives to begin.

10

Why do they play the organ?
Ponderous and sinister,
             it's a thin soul's thunder.
             A fugitive from its fugues
I find a corner of the bar where I sit with my latest love
      – the necromancer, Madam X –
 who sports black nails and a surfeit of nerves
and all her suitors' names inked around her nipples:
             dav gav moz maz
             cynwyd cewydd cornelius colman
             poor tudwg whose chancel has filled with bats
             and Dewi who vanished in a sandstorm.
All sweetwater saints who slept under sallow,
saltwater souls who sailed to the whirlpool.

But the tattoos on this woman are laborious as a suicide note.
Did no one tell her there are words that cannot be written down?
      Yet if vodka and orange make her feel alive
      there must be a miracle in the mix.
That's what the landlord says as he hands us the DVD control
to his Monday afternoon movie –
The Great Escape, of course.
Our favourite part is where Steve McQueen
is caught in the barbed wire

and we zoom in on how he is pinned to the earth
by the totalitarian thorns.

    Oh yes, I think.
    And grin.

And so the aeons pass
    as we allow them to pass
    on the peninsula.

11

This afternoon I find an albatross.
Wounded it has wandered
to lie wide as a windmill
on the tump of Twmpath Tom Brython.
As I look into the well
of its woebegone eye
I see what our sailors never saw –
the shoals dispersed, the icebergs
a paperchain upon a school window.

How she has grown, my wolf-wary child:
she needs no costume now
who is both chooser and chosen,
adding her own milk
to the wave, this shiggly
girl with arms across breasts
which are as white as wheatears,
her habit the surrounding surf,
the salt itself her psalter.

She will betray me I know like all the rest but still I comb her
hair and it is silver down to the root paler even than the stud in
the petal of her ear while her dress is the blue check with that
elderberry stain on the sleeve that won't wash out and she is
such a madam walking always one yard behind on the road to
school past the video shop with all last night's cartridges pushed
through the door and the hairdresser's where already a woman
is bent double with damp strands over her face and although we
hurry we are always late so I give her the money and the white
plastic inhaler and then I am back on Rhych Avenue with the
sea's breath on my neck.

From behind the wall
I watch the scourgers scour the grass:
boys with sticks
come to thump the pumpkin like a big bass drum.

There is nothing so glorious as that gourd,
joined to the earth by its artery,
served at night by a gardener
who has slept there with his thermos.
But as the pumpkin swelled
it grew too huge to hide.

So the children found it.
They touched its skin,
strange as phosphorus.

Amazed
they stroked it
like a breast.

One child corkscrewed out a piece
and tasted it.

Spat out that bread.
Pissed his poisons over it.

Then they stove it with sticks,
wrenched it from the vine,
its eggmeat whitegold as a wedding ring
broken by their boots.

Last they stoned it like a saint,
that new loaf, that god-gourd
grown beyond concealment
but trespassing in someone else's creation.

Now
black snow.
Black kiss
of the eclipse.
   In the garden I stand
before dawn. The black hour. All is gaunt
and ghosted. Ice in the barrel
sighs like a man asleep,
a man who might never wake;
as if sleep is now the silicon in his bones
and the carbon in his heart.
      But such is ice, the foetus
that floats in the ultrascan:
an isthmus in the ocean of its mother.
Now the earth I have dug through the centuries is frozen against me.
      I have come home to a locked house.

Starving, I smash a pane and roust out
a root of horseradish from its holt,
and suck it, earth and all, the sand on it my sugarcane,
bite it, gnaw it, make it my medicine.
To the manna born I am this morning,
its medulla hotting my mouth,
hotter than the host in his wafer
or mead mulled and pokered in a picket fire.
This horseradish loves the soil I sieve and the sand that suckles it.
Where all was barren it is a staff stiff as a burin,
the horseradish that grows in my plot
   – iron cotter pin, dirty sceptre –
      and keeps a beggar warm.

14

Through a waste of winters here's what I recall:
to thrive the soul needs a soul-facing wall.

   Ages ago
      this was a market:
horseradish leaves like flutings of green enamel,
crab apples, salt cod, coneyskins, mussel shells,

remedies for gutrot and the clap,
and the language changing colour
like the stained glass above the chancel in St John's,
cargoes of the tongue unhitched where the sailors caulk the boats,
the pitch blacking the children's clothes.
     You will never get it off,
       the sailors said,
       no matter how hard you rub.

15

I have traced my ancestry back four thousand years
to a family who stood on the ridge
and could feel the storm before they saw it:
          their sky an owl's
egg
              starting to
       crack.

Now from this crest the whirlwind
seems a black enamel lighthouse
rising out of the water
with the sun a prisoner within it:
       so pale and jittery,
       that dying king.

To comfort myself in such weather
I remember that on reaching fifty
Phil Everly gave Don Everly a pound of gold.

Here in the laburnum I count sixteen goldcrests,
imagine sixteen goldcrest hearts,
hear sixteen goldcrest songs.

I listen to the Everly Brothers,
I listen to the goldcrest songs,
but Don Everly does not hang upside down in my laburnum tree.

16

On Judgement Day
I will stand before
a tribunal of trilobites
and justify my life.
Here's what I will say:

Parched, I became what I feared most:
a dry man
stooped to a pool.
But those who pray to salt must pay in thirst.

I drank and went mad
and this is what I learned.
There's a kind of life that scuffles
in the scurvygrass. We are not that.

A walker and a winterer
I never seek but sense the nerve and sinew of the sea.
But must finish where I begin
  – tracing a newel of sandstone
through a greyer level, following a staircase
into the strata to where the change is made:
    different codings,
coolings; whose rocks are fractious children
and the glacier carries centuries in its snout.

I am fallen like the forest in its fanfare of fernfire,
    but always the red
    against the grey,
their atoms in attrition, the scars and sutures
    where an empire ended.

  The seas rose
and flames poured from the wound in the side of the world.
    I drank and went mad
and came eye to eye with myself in the rock.
Because there's no sane man would ever think
    we are what a fossil dreams.

Now sunfish run the tides.
Warmer, warming this shore.

Even here they find their way
– their brass to bless.

Consider the cocklegirl
with her waxpaper cones;
the coins in her satchel, the bite on her neck.
I booked two places on the Skymaster
but she laughed at an old man's whiskery ears.

And I who was bright as the chiton in its mail
must cling to a precipice.

17

Limping along Cwm Befos
I see the winter oak with a fox in its arms
        while beyond is Exmoor
        electric, dark as dulse,
the sunlight leaning like timber in a joiner's yard,
        the shafts
            the spars
        the sweetsawn
            sprucedust
        scattered on the air.

Beyond me the storm is standing out of the sea,
a black bolster whose blade divides the water from the land.
        But already I am leaving,
I who planned the node and name for anemone and nematode,
        already I have started
to disappear.

        And suddenly I see
that the scourgers have tied Christ's
legs. They are beating him with nettles
and the dust of the violet nettleflowers
is settling as a garden at his feet
and the Renaissance is growing out of it
while behind the New Emerald Chinese takeaway
the badlands are awaiting us.
        But step inside:
you'll know mullein's yellow millions
and find fennel's first green to final gold.

Behind me Exmoor
 with centuries
 with centuries

the cocklegirl floating through the dusk
 bearing her tray,
her blue bandanna with the stars upon it,
the moon and sun that govern our griefs.

In the gwter lies galena in a teagreen tier,
the caverns, the cairns, the choruses in coralweed.
This kind of life a walker wears and a winterer weathers.

 Look. There it is:
 the tornado
 like a test tube
 filled with blood.

Even those who have spent millennia in the rock
will have their rousting out.
We are not that.

I drank and went mad –
a saint in the splash zone
haloed with rocksalt.
Now here I am with my thirst beside me,
the last companion.

Yet three glow worms shine in the High Tide Arcade:
the magi's journey has brought them far across the dunes
and into the fair.
 What else can they take from us but
 a mouthful of candyfloss,
 our driftwood cross,
 tickets for the Haunted House?

While beneath the Megablitz
in the terrible tongue
the cocklegirl is counting backwards towards the black zero.
After all I've done for her that's how I'm repaid.

We will vanish together
but each must find his own way out,
must never seek but sense the nerve and sinew of the sea:
    all weathers to wander
    the forbidden places,
    this kind of life
    this kind of life,
    the last of a kind.

Or so says a madman
who forgot his own name.